D1367715

MODERN FRENCH LITERATURE

1870–1940

MODERN FRENCH LITERATURE

1870—1940

by

DENIS SAURAT

KENNIKAT PRESS
Port Washington, N. Y./London

MODERN FRENCH LITERATURE

Copyright, 1947, Denis Saurat
Reissued in 1971 by Kennikat Press
by arrangement with J. M. Dent & Sons Limited
Library of Congress Catalog Card No: 79-103234
ISBN 0-8046-1191-2

Manufactured by Taylor Publishing Company   Dallas, Texas

CONTENTS

MODERN FRENCH LITERATURE—1870–1940

(a) OUTSIDE CONDITIONS

THE Third Republic in France was founded during the disasters of 1870; the German invasion of France revealed two facts: that the imperial regime of Napoleon the Third was incompetent and corrupt; and that the people of France were not attached to it. The republic was in the hearts of the people; and its greatest civilizing task was the education of the people. For the first time in the history of France every village had a school; elementary but sound education was given to the whole people. The State made itself responsible for education, built schools everywhere, made learning free: 'L'instruction est gratuite, laïque, obligatoire'; all had a right to be taught without having to pay for it; religion had no place in the schools; all men and women had a duty to educate themselves. Democracy demands education.

The French language and French literature were given pride of place in the system; all French children had to be taught proper French; all had access to books; all that could pass the necessary examinations could go on with their studies, through the universities, and into careers, without having to pay anything. True democracy was installed in the intellectual domain.

This, which should have been a sound foundation for a true democratic France, split the nation in two.

The moneyed classes looked upon this system as an unendurable attack on their privileges; it so happened that the moneyed classes were also the religious classes: a fact conditioned by the great revolution of 1789–95 and its consequences. The scholastic system of the Third Republic was looked upon by the privileged classes as a method created to destroy religion in the people—which, in some ways, it was. The clergy in France had sided first with the king and the aristocrats against the people; then with Napoleon the Third and the rich classes against the people. Religion had been used by the French Church, since the days of Napoleon the First, as opium for the people. The people now turned against religion, and anti-clericalism became, necessarily, the chief policy of the Republicans. The elementary school-teachers of the new system were anti-clericals, and brought the children up to regard religion and the priests as enemies of the people.

Naturally, the moneyed classes reacted. Against the elementary schools that taught the poorer people little could be done: strangely enough, no money was forthcoming from the rich to teach the poor—even to teach the poor religion and submissiveness. So the Republicans had their way with the people. But the bourgeoisie did manage—although in a mediocre manner—to create enough schools in the secondary sphere to educate its own children in a religious and anti-democratic way. The Republicans, tied by their own doctrine of freedom for all, and not daring to oppose the formidable money powers in this special field, allowed thus a system of *écoles libres*, which meant religious schools, to arise for a middle and upper class public. Some careers, especially the permanent places in the army and navy, became the preserves of these bourgeois-educated young men. This was to play a great part in the events from 1939 to 1940 and the fall of France: in a great many cases there was no contact at all between the leaders, brought up by the priests, and the people, brought up by the Republican, anti-clerical, and by now largely Communist teachers. The military leaders and the people mistrusted each other very deeply, and the whole collapsed under the German impact, even as in 1870—in corruption and incompetence.

Yet the republic had survived the war of 1914–18: at that time the effects of these facts had not yet developed; the spiritual cleavage had not reached so deeply at the time of the First World War. Neither side had gone so far as yet: the bourgeois classes were not Fascist but liberal-minded about

1910; and the working classes were hardly Socialists as yet. The 1914–18 war precipitated the antagonism; Russia on the one hand, Italy on the other brought into the open ideologies that had only been latent before 1918, and which would probably have never been worked out fully in France otherwise.

The great scandals and their results weighed much in the formation of public opinion. But the Panama scandal, the *affaire* Boulanger, and the Dreyfus affair were given solutions that, on the whole, were satisfactory to the masses. The corruption of financial circles was exposed and at least in part punished in the Panama affair; General Boulanger failed to establish a military dictatorship; Dreyfus, in the end, was proclaimed innocent. So before 1914, there was a prevalent feeling in the masses that justice did exist. After the Stavisky scandals, before 1939, that feeling had disappeared.

Literature partly mirrored, and partly submitted to, those various influences and events.

The dichotomy within the soul of the nation was mirrored spiritually in the opposition, in fact, between the movement represented by Mallarmé and the movement represented by Zola. Symbolism and naturalism in literature were essentially related as opposites, as were clericalism and republicanism. Pro-religious elements actuated a whole school of not very successful critics—Brunetière, Faguet, Lemaître—who wrote for the bourgeoisie. Against them, Anatole France represented the truly popular attitude. Thus politics were woven into literature proper.

Yet the best kind of literature, from Leconte de Lisle and Mallarmé to Proust and Paul Valéry, had but little to do with politics; and in that domain of pure literature, the French, during this turbulent and not very creditable period, 1870–1940, achieved perhaps the greatest success of all their national activities. Perhaps posterity will remember best what the French did best.

After all, even the glorious reign of Louis XIV is not so glorious when looked at by the historian proper. But

Molière and Racine remain. Thus the best of what lies behind religion can be found in Mallarmé and in Valéry, who are irreligious. The best of what lies behind anti-clerical rationalism is found in Anatole France, whose scepticism saps rationalism as insidiously and deeply as it does official religion.

Meredith, in the *Essay on Comedy*, compares the spirit of France facing her enemies to a god confronted in fight by a giant. The giant strikes and apparently his formidable mace goes through the god, yet the god is not destroyed and the giant does not understand. Thus what can be killed of France is not the best part of her.

(*b*) INNER DEVELOPMENT

In some aspects the years from 1870 to 1940 constitute a definite period in French literature, and even in world literature. From some other points of view there are no periods in literature, but a chronology of great men's works. What are schools? Mallarmé was a teacher rather than a master: he was better at telling people what to do than at doing it himself; he was chiefly good at telling people what not to do. That is why his influence was so great. A teacher may have a school. A master kills a school, because he produces a perfect masterpiece, which thereafter can only be imitated, and imitation is death. After Racine there is no French tragedy. Shakespeare's faults gave his successors a chance, but even so they could not take it, and there is no great English drama after Shakespeare, nor Greek after Euripides, and so on. A new genius has to create something new.

Nevertheless, it is useful to clarify our thoughts and think in terms of periods, because our perception of great men needs a background. Hugo is in the Romantic period. He was really a fake Romantic; his genius lay elsewhere: in epic force and in sarcastic realism. The Romantic period deformed him as it distorts our view of him. Yet we would not truly 'register' Hugo if we did not see him *in* the Romantic period.

Now Mallarmé began expressing himself soon after 1870 and the new period derives its new colour from him and his co-workers, Verlaine chiefly. But Mallarmé never really succeeded. Yet his disciple Valéry succeeded and was in 1940 the official poet of the Third Republic. From 1925 his reign is established and concurs with that of Proust and Gide. None of the younger men who appeared before 1940 really unseated this trinity. But Valéry is only Mallarmé made into success. Mallarmé from 1875 to 1890 and Proust from 1920 to 1930 are the two focal points on which the period moves. What is the relationship between them? They proceed from the same mentality applied in different fields. Both repudiate the classical view of the predominance of reason and the romantic view of the predominance of feeling. For both, the world as we perceive it is a distortion of the true world, which remains inaccessible. For both, the true mission of literature is to reveal, beyond what we see and hear and feel, glimpses of that world of super-reality which is the only reality. Mallarmé the poet deals mostly with the external world of sensory perception, and shatters it and tries to see beyond it. Proust the prose writer, the 'novelist,' deals mostly with the internal world, the self, which is also a distortion, and behind the failures, the intermittences of the self and the feelings, tries to obtain glimpses of something eternal. But Mallarmé agrees with Proust about the self being illusory, and about love being illusory.

> Réfléchissons . . .
>   ou si les femmes dont tu gloses
> Figurent un souhait de tes sens fabuleux,
>   (*L'Après-midi d'un faune*)

and Proust agrees with Mallarmé that flowers are

> Des avalanches d'or du vieil azur.

Proust describes flowers so as to show us behind them, even better than Mallarmé can, 'une certain réalité spirituelle—devant les clochers de Martinville,' 'certains arbres d'une route de Balbec.'

Both Mallarmé and Proust mistrust the intellect, the feelings and our perception of the outside or inside world: What is left? Sensation. The actual impact on our senses, hearing, sight, or the heart: not the feelings or the ideas aroused by this impact: feelings and ideas are both baseless, arise from misinterpretations. But the impact on our senses is a fact. Intellect, feeling, are groundless: sensuality is, in itself, something. A base doctrine? Sometimes. But at other times, a sensation comes to us from the higher world: if we can control our feelings and rein in our minds, then we make contact with the eternal, though very rarely.

'Ce plaisir particulier que j'avais quelquefois éprouvé dans ma vie," says Proust. 'Cette qualité inconnue d'un monde unique.'

'Tel qu'en lui-même enfin l'éternité le change,' says Mallarmé. Thus runs the expansion of the search for the highest from Mallarmé to Proust and Valéry, from 1870 to 1940, from the beginning to the end of that Third Republic, in some ways the grossest, in some ways the subtlest of all the modes and phases of French history.

But a mood never covers a whole nation; and a previous mood never wholly dies out of the soul.

Along this 'modern' line Mallarmé–Proust–Valéry, several other lines run; sometimes in a blend, sometimes separate. The Naturalism of the previous period is in full bloom. Zola reigns until his death in 1903. The influence of the line Flaubert–Zola throughout the world is astonishing. The world had taken but little notice of greater and more famous Frenchmen; Hugo and Lamartine never really impressed the two continents as Flaubert and Zola did. Novels were written from Yokohama to Chicago on the Zola model, and still are. Strange that at the same time poems should be written in the same places on the Mallarmé model. Zola is the Mallarmé of the mob: he also believes in sensation and in nothing else, being a scientific materialist. There is much of Zola in Proust. But there are other, older survivals. The Romantics are fully alive. Rostand and Madame de Noailles and Romain Rolland are Romantics; and very good Romantics too. Jules Romains and Georges Duhamel are synthetic products, in whom you can find all kinds of art artistically and artfully mixed. And what is Anatole France? And what is Péguy? They derive from further back still, from Voltaire, from Bossuet: perhaps the two final ancestors of all French minds; some Voltaire colouring all French prose; some Bossuet colouring all French poetry.

Mallarmé could find in Bossuet the sense of the mysteries and the contempt of this world. Proust could find in Voltaire the early prototypes of Mme de Guermantes and M. de Charlus; and much scepticism about the value and durability of the self.

Then, as the Republic began to sink towards the last and most terrible of France's wars, some younger men appeared in a shouting and heroic mood—men like Aragon, Malraux, Montherlant, Chamson, Céline—many others. They felt the ship was going down. We heard them shout out, and sometimes swear. They are symptoms of great energy; they have over-come Mallarmé and Proust. Will their work and that of even newer ones, mature in the new world? That will be for the next historian to say. But there is plenty of hope. In our period, in any case, France lived up to her old reputation: her literature impressed and ruled the world. No absolute master of supreme genius appeared: no Hugo, no Balzac, no Molière. But at no time had the nation thought so much about art and literature, nor produced such quantities of very good art and literature, among, of course, much of inferior quality.

The poets, when they exist (I am thinking of the eighteenth century—a great century with no poets), give us the essential spirit of their time. Let us begin with them. Mallarmé must be our first subject; but as nothing ever begins at any precise time, we have preliminary fragments of Mallarméism in Rimbaud and in Baudelaire—on whom a few remarks are necessary.

BAUDELAIRE is a forerunner of the new French poetry: from some angles he is also the best of the later poets, in spite of great lapses; but he belongs to a previous period and is really a Romantic, though often an inverted one. Verlaine is in many ways the nearest the French have produced to the English idea of a true poet; he cannot be termed new or old; but although he expressed the ideas of the Symbolists better than any one else, they were for him only a phase; all schools are represented in him; yet, like all true lyricists, he was also at heart a Romantic. Something truly new begins to be evident in Rimbaud: something hard, cruel, unjust, unromantic, a new departure of genius cutting off the past. Rimbaud was born in the Ardennes, in the harsh north-east of France, and there is much of the barbarian in him, much of the Nietzschean wrecker of Christianity; before Nietzsche, he was both more sincere and more deceitful than Nietzsche. At seventeen he had a passionate friendship with Verlaine, whom he both admired and despised, ran away with him to London, exasperated him so violently in Brussels that Verlaine was moved to try and shoot Rimbaud. Poor Verlaine had to do two years in a Belgian prison, and on coming out and trying to join Rimbaud in a Rhineland village, was thrashed mercilessly by him and left in a ditch. Exit Rimbaud; but nothing could cure Verlaine, whose unrequited passion tailed off in drink, poetry, religion, wickedness, and the hospitals.

All this is highly symbolical: what Rimbaud did to Verlaine (who richly deserved it) Rimbaud did to French poetry, which has never recovered either. (Except that Paul Valéry can be considered as a sane interlude.)

Rimbaud died twice: to literature at nineteen and to life at thirty-seven. Verlaine resuscitated, or rather, suscitated him in 1885 by his *Poètes maudits*. Rimbaud wrote before Mal-

larmé, but had his effect and fame after Mallarmé. At nineteen he gave up literature, left Europe, and tried to make
money—in which he partly succeeded—but an untimely death
stopped him. Yet between sixteen and eighteen he wrote
three of the best poems in the French language—or any
other: *Le Bateau ivre*, *Les Chercheuses de poux*, *Voyelles*;
134 lines altogether. Most of them could have been written
by Victor Hugo, with a little more realism and much less
good temper. 'Le rut des Béhémot et des maelstroms
épais' in *Le Bateau ivre* is related to

> Le rut religieux du grand chêne cynique

in *Le Satyre*; and to the comet of *Là-haut* in the second *Légende*.

> Je regrette l'Europe aux anciens parapets,

though good, is not so good as

> Le vieil anneau de fer du quai plein de soleil

in Hugo's *Pauvres Gens*.

It is rather by what he gave up than by what he achieved
that Rimbaud had a great influence, first of all on Verlaine
and Mallarmé. He gave up the would-be perfection of
Leconte de Lisle as a mere pose; he gave up clarity; he gave
up this world in his search for another; logically enough he
then gave up literature. He cultivated concentration of
expression and of feeling in *Les Illuminations*, and then gave
up formal poetry and wrote *Une Saison en Enfer* in prose to
concentrate still further: he gave up meaning; he tried to
give up the use of words that had already been used. Poetry,
or literature, in his last phase, was an attempt to say nothing
but what was new, to bring together only words that had
never been together before.

Then he gave everything up. What he had been looking
for, no one can tell. He could not, unless it were

> Silences traversés des mondes et des anges
> O l'Oméga, rayon violet de ses yeux.

Mallarmé is in many ways an explanation of Rimbaud. Not
that Mallarmé started from Rimbaud. Mallarmé was the

older, and the earlier, and the better thinker.   But in Mallarmé some sort of explanation is found of what Rimbaud
became too impatient to explain.

The consummation of Rimbaud is in Mallarmé; his paternal
origin is in Baudelaire (his maternal origin is only Victor
Hugo: in Rimbaud's brain a fusion of Baudelaire and Hugo
took place).   Indeed, the beginning of modern French literature, of what is specifically 'modern' in it, is in Baudelaire,
and more precisely in Baudelaire's *Correspondances*.

> L'homme y passe à travers des forêts de symboles
> Qui l'observent avec des regards familiers —
> Les parfums, les couleurs et les sons se répondent.

Even the faults of the coming poets are indicated; they will
only too often imitate nature, since, says Baudelaire,

> La Nature est un temple où de vivants piliers
> Laissent parfois sortir de confuses paroles.

Words mixed up and not to be understood come, and then
only sometimes, from nature.   But the poets soon were to
do better: their words remained *confuses paroles*, in fact,
became more and more confused; but they forgot the *parfois*;
they did it all the time.

MALLARMÉ earned his living, very modestly, as a teacher of English in various French State schools. He was a bad teacher, and he did not know English any too well. But he loved English poetry, and he loved even Edgar Allan Poe, whose poems he translated, and transformed. It is conceivable that his high notion of poetry came from this situation: poetry was for him something that you do not understand perfectly, because poetry for him was first of all English poetry, which he did not understand perfectly. But his imagination supplied his want, and thus produced what was better than his starting-point, sometimes. Occasionally, however, the full glory came through. He used to receive his friends on Tuesday evenings in a small flat in the rue de Rome in Paris and talk to them, and he was poetry to them: a master of never fully comprehended mysteries. No one who went ever forgot.

Another association of Mallarmé's which is not made enough of is Provence. He was for a while teacher of English at Tournon and for seven years in Avignon, and he was a friend of Aubanel and of the great Mistral. This was probably also one of the sources of his high values: Provençal poetry is mysterious to the French, being much nearer to instinct than French poetry ever is. So when he came to Paris at thirty, by formation he was not really French, but Anglo-Provençal. That is why he had so much to teach the French, whose tradition was eloquence rather than poetry, and had, in any case, become sterile by 1870. Mallarmé died prematurely, with his work hardly begun (most of Hugo's great work was done after the age at which Mallarmé died)—of a curious illness: a constriction of the throat now well known and easily cured.

Mallarmé expresses, in fragmentary flashes, the spirit of a new kind of literature, which most cultured people consider the only true literature, and which in any case, dominates the period from 1870 to 1940. Mallarmé's thinking makes the Romantic period appear tawdry—with, of course, some exceptions, rather too brilliant—not exceptions of men, but, in each great man's work, exceptions of a few successful lines here and there. Mallarmé also causes us to feel at times that the classical period had somehow missed the very idea of what literature was, and very specially of what poetry was. Of course, the really great men of the seventeenth century occasionally reached the level of their own greatness, but they did not reach it of set purpose; they did not know where their own greatness lay.

Now several poets had already known something of the true essence of poetry, but none of them had been sufficiently powerful of intellect to put together a coherent conception of poetry. By a miracle which is in the nature of the act of creation, practice had come before theory. Unknown to Mallarmé, Blake had already produced a body of poetry which neither Mallarmé nor any of his successors could equal, either in quality or in quantity. But practically no one knew of Blake. Poe had had a glimpse of most of the Mallarméan ideas, but had spoilt them both in his theoretical expression and in his own attempts in verse or prose. Nevertheless, Poe had become a naturalized Frenchman at the hands of Baudelaire—which the English much resent—and Mallarmé himself tried to see whether in French Poe's poems could not be made into poetry. In France, Gérard de Nerval, Baudelaire, and Rimbaud were all stepping-stones of the intellect towards Mallarmé. They had at times seen things in a true light, but Mallarmé was the first man to see things clearly, coherently, and permanently.

Mallarmé's central idea has a negative and a positive side. Most of his disciples have seen clearly enough the negative principle, but few have understood or accepted, and even fewer have put into practice, the positive principle. Let us have the master's own words: 'Abolished, the intention, aesthetically an error, although it directs nearly all masterpieces, of enclosing into the subtle paper of a book anything else than, for instance, the horror of the forest, or the silent thunder diffused in the leaves: not the intrinsic and dense wood of the trees. A few jets of intimate glory truthfully trumpeted, evoke the architecture of the only inhabitable palace; not any stone.' (*Vers et prose*, Perrin, p. 184.)

Mallarmé's great handicap is that he cannot write, either in prose or in poetry: he is a thinker and a talker, not a writer; this fatal fault has also descended to many of his disciples, in whom the talker only survived. Therefore Mallarmé has to be explained and is meat for the professor.

'Not the intrinsic and dense wood of the trees.' The wood is not poetry: reality is not art. Anything that tells a tale is not poetry. Anything that teaches a lesson is not poetry. Anything that expresses feeling is not poetry—'The silent thunder diffused in the leaves.' Let your thunder be silent: out goes Hugo. Drama? A tale told by an idiot, full of sound and fury, signifying nothing. Drama is the least poetic of all forms of writing. Out goes Shakespeare; but more especially out goes Racine. Molière had the good sense not to pretend to be a poet. Note *signifying* nothing. The sound and the fury *mean* something, but they *signify* nothing. They mean the feelings that cause them; and that is not literature. To *signify* something, to achieve literature, you have to go beyond the real, and create a sign of eternal things. This leads to the positive principle in Mallarmé. He destroys all previous literature, apart from some exceptional passages. What then does he create?

The world as we know it, as we see and hear it, is a distortion of the real world, which is eternal. The function of poetry is to restore the eternal. Luckily the logical world as we know it is incomplete, incoherent, because it is a distortion of the true world. The poet's business is to spot the cracks in the fabric of things as we see them; and to widen the cracks and penetrate beyond reality to the eternal. The true palace, the only palace that can be lived in, is on the other side of the stones. But the cracks are not in the stones:

they are in the logic of the mind that put the stones together.
Nothing—to be negative again for an instant—is so deceitful
as a perfect form: it attempts to hide the cracks. Out go
Leconte de Lisle and the Parnassians. Perfection of form
is not poetry.

But what do we penetrate to? Not an idea, very specially
not an idea. Ideas are that logic of the false world we live in.
We must by-pass ideas, and create, with words, an opening
into the spiritual world. A sure test that we have failed is
that we understand. What we understand cannot be true.
The spiritual world is made up of things and beings that we
cannot understand. Poetry is the only method that can lead
us into the spiritual world. Philosophy can only *talk* about
the eternal and therefore distort it; poetry can create an
impression which *is* eternal: it bears this hall-mark, that
you cannot understand it and yet feel it.

Hence the true subjects of poetry will be the failures of
reality: *Les Fleurs du Mal*—evil, vice, illness, shortcomings
of all kinds: *La Nuit d'Idumée*. But Baudelaire's great fault
was too much concreteness: you must not describe the crack,
you must go through it.

'Pour qu'en émane, sans la gêne d'un concret rappel, la
notion pure' (*Vers et prose*, p. 189). 'Quelque éclair suprême,
d'où s'éveille la Figure que nul n'est' (p. 214). The emana-
tion of a pure notion, without the embarrassment of concrete
reminiscences. A supreme flash from which is aroused
that Shape that no one is.

'Tel qu'en lui-même enfin l'éternité le change.' We know
the poet here below as he is not, distorted. Once dead, he
becomes his true self, which we cannot know.

Poetry thus overtakes music. Music can create in us that
impression of the eternal, arouse the shape that no one is,
beyond our understanding: what we understand in music is
not music. Why then write poetry? Because music is too
simple: the sounds it uses have no meaning to begin with.
Therefore music cannot give up meaning; and it is by the
giving up of meaning that we penetrate into the eternal world;

it is by the giving up of ourselves that we reach God. Poetry muSt recover its true role, that music has usurped too easily. 'La poésie doit reprendre son bien à la musique.' Music is made by the poets out of words that had a meaning, not out of meaningless sounds, and the poets' music is in the other world, of which the musicians reach only the threshold.

Our sensations, not only of hearing—another superiority of poetry over music—but of perfumes, colours, images, taSte even, and sensuality, are perceptions of some unknown aétion from the other world—as Blake might say to some unknown god:

For thou haSt touched my five senses and they answered thee.

So words are the symbols of sensations that are the symbols of inaccessible realities; a symbol which is underStood is no longer a symbol.

Now all this, told by the hour from the height of Mallarmé's mantelpiece as he leaned on it and held forth to amazed disciples—among whom was Paul Valéry—was a wonderful experience, and none that heard it forgot the experience though they forgot the lesson. But in faét, in the aétual gold of published poems, what did it amount to? To very little. This, the higheSt ideal of poetical imagination, was self-deStruétive. In faét, there was literally nothing that one could write about. Mallarmé had set a problem, like the squaring of the circle, or perpetual motion, which no one could solve. No one had solved it in the paSt; Mallarmé himself could set it but not solve it; no one after him solved it. Mallarmé pointed out that true poetry, in the paSt, had only been produced by accident, as a by-produét, while the writer was engaged in some pursuit which he thought was the making of poetry but which was not. Mallarmé did not think much of his own poetry, and explained to his disciples that he was secretly engaged in writing an *epos*, his true work, which never saw the light; and one rather shudders when imagining what Mallarmé would have thought of the work that came after him.

Poetry is by its very essence a failure; from each poet a

few lines survive as successful, as a true echo from a higher
world, produced in the poet no one knows how. The
writing of poetry is practically impossible.

Mallarmé is no exception. His poems can easily be printed
in some fifty pages, and are mostly bad. The worst kind of
Baudelairean romanticizing is in

> Une négresse par le démon secouée

The worst kind of Boileauesque platitude is in

> Une veille t'exalte à ne pas fermer l'œil

(a line which would have been rejected from *Le Lutrin*)
and the worst kind of Mallarméan incomprehensibility is in

> O la berceuse, avec ta fille et l'innocence
> De vos pieds froids, accueille une horrible naissance,

the worst kind because Mallarmé means something very
simple and deliberately makes it incomprehensible because
of his theories. He means he has sat up all night writing,
and his wife has cold feet and his daughter too, but they are
nice people, and will they welcome his poem, which is
horrible—and no doubt get up and make coffee? All this
may be the symbol of something incomprehensible, but do
we really care?

There remain, perhaps, in all some thirty lines (and I am
being generous) which are genuinely immortal, and will give
a dreary immortality to the fifty pages. A price we pay
gladly, however, to have

> Ce peu profond ruisseau calomnié, la mort,
> Je t'apporte l'enfant d'une nuit d'Idumée,
> Des avalanches d'or du vieil azur, au jour
> Premier et de la neige éternelle des astres
> Jadis tu détachas les grands calices,

and some two dozen lines or so besides.

How can one say nothing and yet re-create the eternal?
Yet it was necessary, in the evolution of culture, that all this
should have been thought and said. Literature will go on
telling tales, staging dramas, expressing feelings, drawing a
moral and occasionally touching heaven. But now we know

that, except occasionally, literature is a second-rate achievement. The first-rate has to come from heaven, and we can
feel it but not understand it.

They called it Symbolism and left it (as again, Blake had
said, after Revelation, about Egypt). That ferocious and
cynical individual whom deluded fools called sometimes poor
old Verlaine, and who could write when Mallarmé couldn't,
put it all quite simply into an *Art poétique* in 1874:

> De la musique avant toute chose;

out goes the meaning:

> Il faut aussi que tu n'ailles point
> Choisir tes mots sans quelque méprise;

out goes the grammar, as Verlaine writes, on purpose making
a mistake:

> C'est des beaux yeux derrière des voiles;

(but out goes poetry, too, with the grammar).

> Prends l'éloquence et tords-lui son cou;

another mistake in grammar, but out goes Hugo:

> Oh! qui dira les torts de la Rime?

(Boileau, of course, in a very good satire), but who can resist

> Quel enfant sourd ou quel nègre fou
> Nous a forgé ce jouet d'un sou
> Qui sonne creux et faux sous la lime?

Who indeed, but Verlaine himself, whose rhymes are excellent,
and as for his wit:

> Fuis du plus loin la Pointe assassine,
> L'esprit cruel et le rire impur;

but he, Verlaine, revelled in all that—ferocious wit and foul
laughter, as he owned himself to be

> Lucullus? non, Trimalcion.

Yet, contradicting himself and all that, Verlaine reaches true
Symbolism, and oftener than Mallarmé perhaps.

> Le poisson, pour servir au Fils de monogramme,
> Quelque chose du cœur enfantin et subtil,
> Des signes fous auxquels personne ne répond.

But Verlaine became too easy; a dreadful facility descended on all the disciples and imitators of Mallarmé and Verlaine. Even the Romantics sank no lower, and indeed the late Romantics and the late Symbolists sink together into the same morass.   At least Mallarmé died in time, and Rimbaud went away to Abyssinia in time.   But Verlaine had to drink himself to death.   Yet some critics call these three only the forerunners of Symbolism.   Symbolism died before its fore-runners, but its shadow, and its shade, still cover and haunt all poets to-day, and the greater number of prose writers. Mallarmé and his band, besides producing a few specimens of good poetry, taught all their successors that some things, until then thought to be first-rate, were not literature; and also in what direction good literature lay; and all writers ever since have been a little ·in doubt about themselves, which is good for writers, and yet not too good.   Neither Shakespeare nor Hugo were in doubt, I fancy.   But after 1900 or so, all honest writers wondered what Mallarmé would have thought of them.

THE OPPOSITE POLE—ZOLA: 1840–1903

It is curious to find Zola associated with the south by his origins—even as Mallarmé was through his career. Zola had an Italian father and was brought up at Aix en Provence; he came to Paris at eighteen. His great work was really over when in 1898 his sense of justice threw him into the Dreyfus affair: his courageous public letter *J'accuse* is an honour to the French nation and to the human spirit. It is a protest based on the claims of justice alone against tyranny, intrigue, injustice, and stupidity, and it had a decisive effect on public opinion; from then on, the cause of innocence was won against the powers. As every one knows, Dreyfus was falsely accused of being a spy and arbitrarily condemned by army tribunals. Gradually public opinion in France became aware of the wrong done, and under universal pressure the powers that were, after a long fight that split France, had to capitulate. Zola was one of the two or three men who can be said to have won that war. Greater issues than even the vindication of an innocent Jew were involved: the *affaire Dreyfus* brought political power to the parties of the left in France, and was a great step towards democracy. To the clear-sighted (who were very few) it also brought the indication of Germany's intentions and intrigues, and lack of honour, since an honourable German ambassador in Paris was made, unknown to himself, to play the part of a liar by his own Government.

Zola's fighting spirit must be admired; it was also proved further by his dutiful attempts to get into the French Academy; he was a candidate thirty-one times, and always rejected; but he considered it his duty to stand, to vindicate his conception of literature as against the reactionary tendencies of the academicians. Even more than a great writer, Zola was a great man, and the French, rightly, buried him among 'les grands hommes' in the Panthéon. As a last queer parallel with Mallarmé, Zola also died accidentally, from asphyxiation in his bedroom.

Mallarmé may be Proust's father, but Zola is Proust's mother; and perhaps this applies to the whole period. Duhamel also is born out of Zola by Mallarmé, and Céline and Malraux; Mallarmé and Zola are like the two sculptors of Hugo's Moses:

L'un sculptait l'idéal et l'autre le réel.

Zola represents the triumph of materialist science in literature: the very opposite of Mallarmé. For Zola, the real world is the only one. He sees the cracks in it, as well as Mallarmé; but to Zola the cracks do not lead to a higher world; they lead nowhere; they should be stopped; they are the results of man's madness, lack of reason, lack of science. As mankind progresses, the cracks will disappear.

Zola represents, worthily, the prevalent spirit of the Third Republic—scientific materialism. There were fewer believers in France—believers in anything, but especially believers in the national religion, Catholicism—there were fewer believers in 1940 than in 1870. In spite of Catholic revivals—of which more later—the masses have become more and more incredulous. Céline is the latter end of Zola, Céline is the portent at the end, as Rimbaud was the portent at the beginning.

But in Zola's work is seen also, in full, the failure of scientific materialism. The theoretical part of Zola's art is a complete failure. Taine had just published his *Intelligence* in 1870. Virtue was a product of certain conditions; like sugar, perhaps even it was only a by-product. Claude Bernard had explained *la médecine expérimentale*. Everything became experimental. Zola invented *le roman expérimental*. Just as a scientist watches chemicals in their mixtures, or tissues under a microscope, the novelist will watch human beings; and just as a scientist interferes in the course of nature to see what will happen, the novelist will put into the strain of his characters, say, a dose of drunkenness, and see what will happen, as in *L'Assommoir*; or a certain amount of brute sensuality as in *La Terre*, and watch the result.

This kind of novel can only be done by taking in several generations of people, so as to mix the ingredients and see what the next guinea-pig of a character will do, since its mother was this and that, and its father was that and this. And besides, the novelist is liable to be accused of having done it on purpose: the scientist does not *invent* the ingredients he mixes; whereas the novelist does. Therefore the novelist will go to history, and what he invents will be only a parallel to what happened in fact. Hence the naturalist novel is bound to become historical, if it is not to become arbitrary. That is why *Les Rougon-Macquart* will be the natural history of a family under the Second Empire, and will end in *La Debâcle*, the tale of the 1870 war: the inevitable ending of the whole story. Thus the novel approximates to science.

The conditions that command the characters will be physiological, of course, but also social. *L'Assommoir*, *Nana*, *Germinal*, give a picture of social conditions among the lower classes: drink, prostitution, starvation, revolt. And of course Zola is wholeheartedly on the side of social justice, and his most courageous stand in favour of the slandered in the Dreyfus case is in line with his whole thinking. Perhaps Zola had more character than intelligence.

All that part of Zola's work is a literary failure. Yet it truly represents an element that was to gain the upper hand; and if Valéry is more negative, religiously, than Mallarmé, it is because the element of science and pessimism represented by Zola in the 1880s has prevailed in the 1920s, however much of a failure Zola's expression of it may have been. But Zola is not by any means a literary failure. He has his qualities which are unconnected with his systematic thinking, and which make of *L'Assommoir* (1877) and *Germinal* (1885) two masterpieces, two necessary parts of the French literary tradition and of the world literary tradition. Neither Galsworthy nor Sinclair Lewis, nor the *Alexanderplatz*, would have existed without Zola—nor yet Jules Romains. A great man never wholly fails, and where he fails he gives a chance to his successors.

But Zola has qualities of his own that few or none have had to the same degree. He has a sense of life in matter and in forces which is all his own. As a psychologist he is of little use; he does not show us at all well how or why his characters feel inside themselves: they have no inside. But they are moved and carried on by immense external forces that live. Zola needs great mass movements: a big strike, a war. *La Debâcle*, *Germinal*. Once the large crowd of men and women are on the move, Zola's individuals come alive, and behave well and reasonably. Compare the behaviour of Jean in *La Terre*, where he is a stupid fool who does nothing to save himself or his own, with his brave, sensible, and effective action in *La Debâcle*, where the war makes a man of him, although the war is a calamity and a failure, and gives him in the end a new opening. By being integrated into the mass of the nation, he becomes what he failed to be as an individual. But Zola is no nationalist: in *Germinal* the moving external force is the rebellion of the miners. Whereas in *L'Assommoir* the workman is presented as a mere drunkard, although in himself made of good human stuff, in *Germinal*, Étienne and Maheu are two solid sensible workmen. Just as qualities become greater in the mass movements, vices become less important. The sexual *dévergondage* of the miners is fully shown; but Zola shows at the same time the conditions that produce immorality, so that vice appears as a natural force, not as an individual misdemeanour. His lack of individual psychology helps him. The Maheu woman has had her sexual adventures and misadventures; she is nevertheless a good woman, faithful, and useful to both husband and children. Within degradation itself are the germs of goodness and justice; and those in due time will come up, even as through the dirty part of the mould the seeds will germinate and grow and flower. Hence the name *Germinal*: expressing the same faith as in Hugo:

> Le peuple est petit, mais il sera grand.

Zola, astonishingly enough, has a sense of the miraculous. Germs of love and strength exist in the rottenness of mankind: Chaval in *Germinal* is the worst of scoundrels, and yet when he sees Catherine exhausted tenderness is born in him. La Maheude is a soiled heroine, but she has a kind of ferocious loyalty that will mother heroes. Zola has ·suppressed God, but he has scattered the divine qualities all over his human material, and among the worst something which seems to be festering is really germinating. The individual does not matter; why bother so much about his psychology? The forces are at work, and their movement is upwards.

Then, by another paradox, Zola has a deep feeling of responsibility: human nature bears the germs of the future; let us watch and be careful. This is quite against scientific materialism, even as the sense of the miraculous is. But it is Zola's deepest feeling. If we allow justice to go down, we are traitors. Hence his admirable behaviour in the Dreyfus affair; what is a man's life, a novelist's career? Justice must win. Nay, justice will win, whether we help it or not; but if we do not help, we shall be degraded and truly annihilated when justice triumphs. As an atom in that movement of justice, we exist immortally.

This sense of justice becomes a literary quality. Thus in *Germinal* we meet, not only workmen, but engineers, masters, owners, shareholders even. Zola, whose heart is with the workers, is nevertheless just to the others: they are all carried along by uncontrollable forces outside their orbit: the owner is not a wicked man, on the contrary; and he has less happiness in his life than his workmen, who can at least sometimes eat and drink and be merry with the women they have chosen, whereas the master can always eat and drink, but he cannot be merry: a rather childish contrast, yet an effective one. Zola's middle-class families are disarming, so stupid and so comfortable are they; quite incapable indeed of organizing the world in their own interests. *Germinal* does not represent an episode of class-struggle; it pictures human nature on the move, and no amount of merely administrative social changes will change Zola's world. Evil is at the bottom of human life, yet good will spring out of it.

As a good workman, Zola loves the substance on which he works: he wants to help human nature to become better. He feels his work is important. He organizes it well, within each book, within his series of books. The long `Rougon-Macquart` series is architecturally much better thought out and built than Balzac's *Comédie humaine* before or *Les Hommes de bonne volonté* after. Perhaps it is, in fact, too well built, as Jules Romains will insist.

Much has been said against Zola's way of writing French, as a rule in bad faith. Zola very often achieves a simple straightforward way of writing which is not at all an easy exercise. Mostly, as you read him, you forget that he is writing: the objects, the people themselves are before you without the interference of a style; you do not notice his writing. That is a proof of excellence: if it were bad, you would notice it. His style is only his subject-matter naturally displayed before you in its details: and that is great art.

THE REACTION AGAINST ZOLA: RELIGION AND PHILOSOPHY

In 1887 the *Figaro* published a *Manifeste des Cinq contre la Terre* for which the Five, all disciples of Zola, and not one of them worth his little finger, were sorry in the after years. Yet the protest was necessary. *La Terre* was to have been the novel of the French peasant, and is a failure. The French peasant, a universal favourite in politics and in legend—though not in economics—has had bad luck with the novelists. Balzac's *Les Paysans* is a great book, but it presents the peasant as a ferocious savage, worthy of Fenimore Cooper in his anti-Redskin moods, but with none of the endearing traits of the Mohicans. Balzac did not know the peasant; neither did Zola; neither did the Five, who did not care for the peasant, but merely accused Zola of obscenity, which, they said, was not art.

About the same time Brunetière was becoming famous by

trumpeting *la faillite de la science,* the bankruptcy of scientific materialism. Paul Claudel had become converted to Catholicism in 1886, as Verlaine had done in prison in 1874 and Péguy was to do later, following Léon Bloy.

Mallarmé and the Symbolists oscillated on the brink of Catholicism and some of the disciples went over.. They produced a lot of noise rather than a real effect. In the end the spirit of Zola was too strong for them, and in Mauriac, for instance, there is more of Zola than true Catholics like. The failures of Catholicism rather than Catholicism became the subject of literary essays: Léon Bloy is really a condemnation of Catholics, as is Péguy, as is Bernanos with *La Grande Peur des bien pensants.* And I cannot see that a single great work of art came out of the Catholic revival, whose trumpets sounded loud because of the surrounding empty spaces. Some good essays like Maritain's; some bad poems, like Claudel's. But Proust, Gide, and Valéry were not affected. Anatole France merely laughed, and that was quite enough; as for Céline— he is much worse than Zola.

Jules Lemaître, Maurice Barrès, as Catholics, were fakes; they did not believe. Neither did Brunetière. As for Charles Maurras, he did not even condescend to pretend, as the others pretended, and got himself excommunicated—but excommunicated from what, since he was not a Catholic? It is his Catholic readers that were excommunicated.

A much deeper movement was beginning in a fundamental layer: Bergson was beginning a creative evolution towards true religious ideas and no longer, as Brunetière or Barrès, towards a use of bad religion as a camouflage for bad politics. Bergson's first essay, *Sur les données immédiates de la conscience,* was published in 1889. It gradually became possible for a reasonable man to own that he was a religious man. Bergson's great influence did not really begin before the *Évolution créatrice* (1907), and in the same year Hamelin published his epoch-making essay *Sur les éléments principaux de la représentation,* which is a demonstration of the existence of God. Bergson has had a great influence on literary men, who do not understand him very well; but little on professional philosophers, who, on the contrary, have been profoundly moved by Hamelin. Hamelin cannot write at all, and has not touched literary men; yet he represents the true French tradition of Cartesian intellectualism, whereas Bergson's criticism of the intellect is not really in keeping with French feeling. But Bergson can write a little, at least he can be read; whereas Hamelin cannot. Bergson is a true Symbolist and looks for reality, as Mallarmé did, above the world of sense and mind. Hamelin is a pure classic, who trusts in the mind alone. Bergson is tentative and convinces you that there may be a God; Hamelin is positive and says there is a God. It is quite an experience for the serious-minded to read one after the other those two books of 1907: *L'Évolution créatrice* and Hamelin's essay. A true impression of the highest intellectual achievements of France cannot be gained unless Hamelin is read as well as Bergson. If religion in France has again become intellectually respectable and possible it is owing to Hamelin even more than to Bergson. Somehow the period was not attuned to religion. The deepest thinking of the time was truly religious, in Bergson and Hamelin; but their religious feeling did not produce literature as it had done in Pascal or Bossuet: no great religious orator appeared. Lacordaire, in the Romantic period, is the last one we have heard of.

The professed Catholics, mostly converts, blustered tremendously, in the newspapers of the political right; but in the literary sphere Léon Bloy, Péguy in prose, Paul Claudel, Francis Jammes in poetry are the only names that deserve consideration; with, in the latter novel, Bernanos and Mauriac. None of them are first-rate as writers. Péguy was a great man, and a great soul. He was hardly a master of prose, although he achieves passages of a certain kind of genius. Perhaps journalism was the downfall of the literary Catholics: the aggressive bluster of Maurras and Daudet is connected with that of Léon Bloy, a very unpleasant polemist, and even of Péguy who spoils by shouting the effect of some wisdom.

Bernanos could have been a great novelist, had he been primarily a novelist, just as Péguy could have been a great essayist: both fail by devoting space and energy to a virulent condemnation of people whom we do not care about either way—thus they fall out of literature—Claudel also might have been a poet, had he not swollen his style with a would-be impressive rhetoric, which is only boring. How pretentious is the simplicity of Francis Jammes!

Of course the Catholics came to life in an unfavourable atmosphere. Zola and France were the universal favourites when the Catholics began and insisted overmuch: the public felt that it was being imposed upon and did not really respond; unliterary novelists like René Bazin and Paul Bourget had great sales among the conservative bourgeoisie; they could be, and were, read by well-brought-up young ladies. Mauriac, at the end of the period, is a much quieter writer, and therefore has a better chance. Less gifted perhaps than Bernanos, he achieves more penetrating effects. We shall meet some of those names again in our course; but they had to be mentioned together here as part of a movement that failed. As individuals, and in patches, some succeeded to a certain extent.

THE INDUSTRIALIZATION OF THE NOVEL

THERE fall within our period chronologically quite a number of novelists that were famous for quite a long time, and that have many merits—also novelists that will give the leisured and cultured classes—should there ever be such classes again —quite a lot of pleasure. They are rapidly becoming old-fashioned. But have we not seen Jane Austen and Trollope become semi-fashionable again? In France, an abundant flowering came from the seeds that had not grown in Flau bert's rather restricted garden. The seeds were all there, but Flaubert had no time to attend to them, and no space to give them reality. Hence Daudet, Maupassant, the Goncourts, Huysmans, and later Hervieu, Hermant, Marcel Prévost, René Bazin, Paul Bourget, Henri Bordeaux even, and many others. A rather wearisome list; and it is difficult to get excited about any of them.

They are not particularly disciples of Flaubert, they are rather left-overs. None of them reaches greatness; most of them have produced one or two volumes that give pleasure to a cultured reader. Several of them have had rather tremendous reputations that are now seen to have been inflated, and are now perhaps deflated overmuch. Hundreds and thousands of volumes of novels constitute a sort of jungle in which patient hunters may find occasional good quarry, if they are prepared to sample and reject many specimens on short trials.

The matter rather grows beyond the literary sphere and becomes nearly an economic and social question, in which literature provides only one of several elements.

During the Romantic period, poetry was the dominant *genre*. A novelist was definitely a rather despicable proletarian in that snobbish world. Not much difference was made between Eugène Süe and Balzac. Balzac had a very hard fight against the critics and the press, but he succeeded, through sheer genius and enormous quantity, in establishing the novel as literature. But, even as Eugène Süe, Balzac was already an industrialist; so was Alexandre Dumas, who ran a regular novel-factory, in which he had employees working to order under his signature. The novel grew in popularity, and, nevertheless, in dignity. *Eugénie Grandet* was praised as a seventeenth-century classic. *La Cousine Bette* was an undoubted masterpiece of the front rank.

Then came Flaubert, who gave final *lettres de noblesse* to the novel by working at each sentence as Racine had worked at each one of his couplets.

But meanwhile various calamities were occurring in other domains of literature which finally left the novel as the only living variety in the jungle.

Lyrical poetry, the great romantic *bête fauve*, died out, like the sabre-toothed tiger who died out for lack of prey. Part of poetry became so platitudinous and so monotonous that it was still printed but was no longer read, except by the uncultured. Another part, on the contrary, became so refined and difficult that few were cultured enough for it: thus Leconte de Lisle and Mallarmé sold by the dozen where Hugo and Lamartine had sold by the thousand dozen.

The drama sank to such decrepitude with highly skilled technicians like Scribe that it really fell out of literature and entered into the category of meretricious shows: part of a certain Parisian industry which is still flourishing; in spite of certain honourable exceptions (no more than honourable— no more than exceptions) the drama stayed in that domain for good and all and is still in it. Then came science.

Science in the seventeenth century had been, as Bossuet had stated truly, in such a category that 'it is not consonant with the dignity of a bishop to meddle in such things' as physics and so on. The eighteenth century had thought twice about that, and Voltaire, who was also a bishop in his own way, had worked hard at Newton. But after Auguste Comte and the 1840s, science had conquered; you had to be 'scientific,' 'positivist,' or you were nothing. Now how

could lyrical poetry or the drama be 'scientific' and 'positivist'?
But the novel could; so said Zola, so said the Goncourts in a
different way.   Sociology was invented by Auguste Comte.
The novelist became a scientific observer of human beings:
Flaubert, who was a doctor's son, rather fancied himself as
an anatomist of man's and woman's feelings.

So the novel scored over the *genres nobles*.

But another transformation was taking place in the reading
public.   The French Revolution had brought to a clear head
a tendency that had been growing throughout Europe in the
eighteenth century, but which gave its full results only after
1870: the extraordinary desire that every human being in a
civilized community should know how to read and write.
Danton and the other monsters of the 1793 variety actually
enacted laws to teach every French child the elements of
learning.   It was a long and painful process, but neither king
nor priest was able to stop it: once the people had understood what was coming, the cause of universal education
went from success to success, and the Third Republic, from
1880 onwards, carried out in full the plans of 1793.

This had most important repercussions in literature.

First of all, throughout the nineteenth century, a huge semi-
cultured public was created.   Of course the millions of
primary school children did not all become omnivorous
readers, but every French man or woman became a potential
reader, and hundreds of thousands made up a reading public
which a hundred years earlier had only been counted in
thousands.   But the culture of these hundreds of thousands
was very low; in fact, they could just read, and knew hardly
anything at all of culture proper.

Poetry demands culture.   Literary drama demands culture.

The novel does not demand culture; 'whoso runs may
read.'   This new illiterate reading class needed feeding; it
could only be fed by the novel.   In the seventeenth and
eighteenth centuries, people actually read Plutarch and Horace
to amuse themselves: how unthinkable!   What percentage
of the reading public nowadays could bear it?   But *Madame*

Bovary or *Les Trois Mousquetaires* amused the nineteenth-century masses.

A special aspect of this phenomenon needs insisting upon: the entry of women—as women—into the reading public. In a way women have always been the great bulk of the clients of literature: the *chansons de geste* in the Middle Ages and the Scudéry novels in the seventeenth century had been composed chiefly for a feminine public. But how restricted, compared to the millions of women who became potential readers after 1850. A *masculine* literature had been offered to a few cultured women throughout the ages; now a literature cunningly designed for women was offered to the feminine masses. Balzac made his literary fortune on women: all the literary critics, as men, to a man, were against him. But the Duchesse de Berry in her prison could hardly bear to wait for the next instalment of a Balzac novel. Balzac had made a tremendous discovery: that a woman, at thirty, could still love and especially be loved—privileges reserved to young girls in previous literature—and the enthusiasm aroused among reading women by that discovery brought untold money and unbounded fame to Balzac. *La Femme de trente ans* is one of his novels; it might be the sub-title of all. *La Comédie humaine* or (as they used to put it) *La Femme de trente ans*. That would have described the goods provided by the firm.

Yet another variety of the female public must be observed; it came to life at the end of the nineteenth century, and made the fortune of René Bazin, Paul Bourget, and many less well-known novelists. The carefully brought up Roman Catholic girl of the bourgeoisie had then to be provided with unimpeachable reading matter. *Esther* and *Athalie* and the sermons of Bossuet, all the masterpieces in which the word *amour* was not mentioned, proved insufficient. After all, the world was moving on, and sooner or later those girls came out, and did manage to read things. So the *familles bien pensantes* began to encourage novels of the Catholic variety, and a great revival of Catholic literature was on the way. Well-to-do uncles who kept several semi-conjugal establishments offered Paul Bourget's novels to their nieces as birthday presents by the hundred thousand, round about 1910.

Between 1910 and 1914, three authors, Paul Bourget, René Bazin—and, for the honour of human nature we are pleased to be able to add—Anatole France, sold some three or four hundred thousand of a new novel. But needless to say, Anatole France went to a different public—though one would be surprised . . .

From Eugène Süe, from the 1830s onwards, fortunes were to be made in the novel. Much of novel-writing then became an industry. Strange, perhaps, that the man who is the pivot of the whole evolution, Flaubert, who is midway between Balzac and Zola, is himself a pure artist, who did not even make a living, who hankered after three thousand francs a year and security. It goes to the credit of human nature that even in mass economics of this kind many individuals remain idealists and put art first. But such were the causes —some of them hardly honourable—that made the novel the dominant species of modern literature. Naturally enough, the greatest number of those who merely exploited the new industry are, or have become, unknown to literature. The serial stories published for decades, and by now more than a century by the newspapers, were produced by hundreds of authors now forgotten; yet Balzac, under the first press magnate, Émile de Girardin, was a writer of serial stories in the daily press, and several of his masterpieces first appeared at the bottom of the pages of infamous rags.

Among the innumerable novelists that flourished—or failed —in this rather tremendous (in quantity at least) production, some should be looked at a little more closely, if only because of their reputation, even if it is of the past.

The two Goncourts, Edmond (1822–96) and Jules (1830–70), perhaps still belong to the future. Their novels are very slow, and their style is over-laboured in a sort of impressionist-pointillist manner. But they have left a *Journal*, and endowed a special Académie Goncourt that is to publish the *Journal*. So far very little has seen the light, and it is to be feared, after two wars and much change, that the public will not perhaps be so terribly impressed when the *Journal* does appear, and reveals what many rather forgotten people did about 1870 or 1880.

Alphonse Daudet (1840–97) is perhaps of most concern to literary-minded readers. He has charm and many interesting subjects; but he altogether lacks power. His superficiality becomes painful when he tackles great problems, such as religious fanaticism in *L'Évangéliste*. Perhaps he is destined to remain a school classic with the *Lettres de mon moulin*. The wit and humour of the *Tartarin de Tarascon* series have largely evaporated. We have seen worse things since then.

Guy de Maupassant (1850–93) has written altogether too many short stories. He has had a great reputation for a long time, but his day is definitely over. Some of his short stories are very good, but in perspective it is becoming doubtful whether the short story is a literary game at all. It may be that it was merely meant by nature and providence to fill two columns in a newspaper in times when paper is cheap and real news insufficient. As for Maupassant's so-called novels, *Une Vie*, for instance, is altogether so dreary and so discouraging that it becomes merely boring. Maupassant is supposed to have exploited fear to the utmost in some of his short stories; his effects are now liable to appear comic.

Huysmans (1848–1907) has had many admirers; probably his conversion to Catholicism is the real cause of his pseudo-importance; nothing in his writings is of any note. His realism is out of date, and his mysticism a fake.

Paul Bourget (1852–1935) is an even worse case. He is altogether without any literary merit whatever, and is only mentioned in warning to unwary readers who might be attracted by his reputation, due entirely to the royalist set of literary critics that perverted all appreciation of French literature in the twentieth century, from Brunetière to Maurras, for, in fact, exclusively political reasons.

Above these and hundreds of even more perishable authors rise, however, some true masters, to be considered more at length and with greater pleasure. Loti, Barrès, and France, before the turn of the century; Rolland, Gide, and Proust, Duhamel and Romains after.

ESOTERIC LITERATURE

This cheapening and spreading of the novel went along with an opposite tendency, or perhaps produced a reaction. One of Paul Valéry's most fruitful *mots* in his *Hommage à Marcel Proust*, when he declares that to him the novel is un-thinkable as a work of art; because of its avoidability. 'When the writer begins—*The duchess arrived at nine o'clock*,' says Paul Valéry, 'I am always tempted to cry: *No, it is not that, it is the countess that arrived, and at eleven*.' A French echo of George Borrow's 'Who would call his book a novel if he could call it anything else?'

Mallarmé certainly did not industrialize himself, and after him, in a sense, true literature becomes esoteric: a thing done by the few, for the very few. A public of one reader, him-self, is Mallarmé's true public. And Valéry's *Monsieur Teste* comes then to the conclusion that it is a weakness to write and even to speak; one is always misunderstood, even by oneself.

The early Gide certainly wrote only for the few.

Yet Proust, in a sort of real though impossible way, managed to unite both contraries: he is both the most esoteric of writers and a determined novelist who will insist on putting his case before the whole world—in a way—as a public. In him these two contradictory tendencies, the cheapening of educa-tion and the over-refinement of ultra-personal sensation, are united, and thus he marks the accomplishment and the end of the period.

LOTI: 1850–1923

LOTI was from the Protestant and seafaring south, and was born at Rochefort. When very young, a Tahitian adventure earned him from South Sea girls the name of a flower of the Pacific islands. He adopted it as his pen-name, and Lieutenant Viaud became Pierre Loti. As a man and a thinker, he hardly existed at all; he went round the earth in a succession of French warships as a sentient mirror of which the French language had miraculously taken possession. He saw the earth and the sea as no one had seen them; and he described them as no one had described them. Nothing could cure the incredible boredom of which he died at the age of seventy-three, leaving behind him one of the best palliatives for delicate and melancholy souls averse to intellectual effort.

Loti gives perhaps least rise to controversy among the tale-tellers of his period; he is not even a novelist, he tells tales. Or rather he tells one tale, which he transports, being a sailor by profession, to all quarters of the globe: Iceland, Tonkin, Tahiti, Turkey, Japan, the Basque country, anywhere. His first book on Turkey, *Aziyadé*, in 1879, tells all that Loti has to say, and truly it is rather silly. A young man, a sailor of course as a rule, in a far and very foreign land, meets an unknown, but no doubt beautiful girl; they have a love affair, a wonderful love affair, and then the young man's ship goes (or some such thing happens); the girl dies—how, does not matter—and years after the former young man, now become a mature sentimental philosopher, comes back to visit her grave, and, if occasion offers, her relatives. Thus *Aziyadé*, *Rarahu*, *Le Mariage de Loti*, *Les Désenchantées*. Thus *Madame Chrysanthème*, except that the Japanese girl proves too sordid for the ritual come-back; on the contrary the South Sea island girl behaves in a most admirable way throughout, and her relatives are even better.   For a change in *Ramuntcho* the Basque girl goes into a convent (but then the hero was not a sailor), and in *Pêcheur d'Islande* it is the man that dies (but then both hero and heroine were Bretons, and *Pêcheur d'Islande* is a spotless masterpiece).

In short, Loti's faults are so obvious as to be amusing: he has nothing whatever to say outside the description of people and landscape; no politics for him, no philosophy, no religion. Life is a very sad thing, because people die; especially the people one loves die; but there is nothing to be done about it. Meanwhile how beautiful the world is, how varied, how terrible, how tender, how changeful; how beautiful people are, physically, and morally, or rather immorally, which is the same thing.   How divine the creation is; there may not be a God—though who knows—but there is this Earth and the many various people on it: more than our hearts can cope with, really.

The great pity of the world; the heart-break.   *Pêcheur d'Islande* is perhaps unequalled in sentimentality; but the sentimentality is so pure, so true, so eternal, so simple that the book has an everlasting quality.   The simple hearts of Breton peasants and fishermen; and their hard lives, which to them are quite acceptable if their family affections, their friendships, and their most moderate ambitions are left them.   In a more sophisticated stage of society, all this would be pretence: at this stage where the human beings are only more beautiful, more pathetic animals, the unavoidable truth in the presentation of the elementary but fundamental feelings of human nature makes the book a masterpiece.   Yann, the Breton sailor who dies in an Iceland wreck, has lived a greater and a fuller life than any character in Marcel Proust or André Gide; and Gaud his widow can fill the rest of her life with the kind of suffering that leads to eternity: she has lived.   As for the young boy killed in the Indo-Chinese wars, as for his grandmother in Brittany when she hears of his death—these are of the eternal French people, and if any one wants to know what the French are at bottom, behind the scum of towns

and the rotten politics, let this grandmother of a dead little
peasant sailor tell them.

Mon frère Yves is a curious counterpiĉture: the presentation
of a drunken sailor to whom drink is life; but what a·good
sailor, what a good drunkard, what a good Breton! what a
man, what a sea, what a ship! Conrad has never been so
good, perhaps because he writes of people not his own;
whereas Loti writes of his own people, of himself. Yves is
truly Loti's brother.

But chiefly, what writing, what French! The critic can
do no juŝtice to Loti; quotation can only mangle him. As a
landscape painter he is unequalled. Whether he describes
the port at Conŝtantinople, the mountains of the Basque
country, the terrible cliffs of the French Pacific islands, he
has a range and a power of language, a force of conveying
his impressions such that many of his readers muŝt have
been disappointed when seeing the aĉtual landscapes, Loti
being truly better than the faĉts; and the sea in all its moods
belongs to him: the great northern waves that wrap up Yann
into eternal peace, so that his death is hymeneal to him, or
the full flat sea of the becalmed tropics, and the fogs and the
winds and the sun—they are his.

A curious result of the Romantic period. The seventeenth
century did not appreciate landscape. Then Rousseau discovered the hills; then Chateaubriand discovered the sea; and
the more we discovered the more bored we became. Romantic
landscapes are deadly. Still, literature had discovered nature,
and it became everybody's duty—Hugo's, Flaubert's, even
Zola's—to put in a little description of a landscape whenever
it could be done. But all but the moŝt conscientious readers
skipped those bits, which were inserted to prove that literature had progressed since the seventeenth century (whereas,
of course, it had not)—a sort of trade mark.

And then suddenly, a century later (*Pêcheur d'Islande* is in
1886), here it is: Loti's landscapes are not boring, they are
exciting; nature has come alive at laŝt in literature, in sympathy with simple human feelings that muŝt not be called

romantic, but which the Romantics had also, mostly in vain, tried to describe.

But no one but Loti has ever done it, and therefore no one should try again. Once a thing is done, let it alone. A work of art cannot be repeated; it can only be looked at again and again.

THE INCIDENCE OF POLITICS ON FRENCH
LITERATURE

THERE exists at certain periods a peculiar relationship in France between politics and literature. During the Verlaine and Mallarmé period proper politics did not touch the poets, nor can it be said of Valéry, the true successful representative of that mentality, that he is really concerned in what is called politics. He may allow himself, however, all the philosophical reflections which have a direct bearing on practical affairs, but his sort of philosophizing can hardly be called politics; in any case he himself takes no direct part in affairs. The true relationship of this kind of poet to politics is perhaps essentially expressed by Rimbaud in his youthful purity of spirit, to whom all political men of whatever school are hypocrites and all political so-called 'ideas' are humbug.

But with the 1890s, with the Panama affair and the Dreyfus affair, a new kind of relationship obtains between politics and literature. It is remarkable that Romain Rolland, Maurice Barrès, Anatole France, the three greatest novelists before Proust, each have a middle period which can be called political, in which they devote their talent to the presentation of political problems. It is peculiar also that from the literary point of view, this middle period is their bad period. It is the period of Barrès's *Déracinés*, of Romain Rolland's *Liluli*, of Anatole France's Bergeret. But in all three cases the artist seems to realize his failure and to emerge or try to emerge into a final period which is above politics: Roman Rolland's Indian period, Barrès's *Jardin sur l'Oronte*, Anatole France's *La Révolte des anges*. As political men, as political thinkers they have been failures, and before they die they try to climb back to the artistic heights.

Nor is this phenomenon a new one in French literature. The Second Empire, the period of Leconte de Lisle, Flaubert, Baudelaire, etc., was unfavourable to the entry into politics of

literary men.   But the Romantic period, on the contrary, had
seemed to give great writers their chance in the management
of affairs.   The destiny of Lamartine seems to have a fatal
attraction for the late nineteenth-century writers.   Lamartine
had also begun by being a pure young poet, addicted to
'le culte du moi' as much as ever Barrès was to be.   It was
then in his second period that Lamartine had become a great
political man and been carried to great power in the national
and international fields in 1848, when he was for a few months
the leading spirit of the Second Republic.   It is true that he
fell quickly, in dismal, complete, and permanent failure, but
no doubt each new ardent spirit believes that it can win the
success and avoid the subsequent failure.   Whereas probably
the life of Lamartine proves that the writer is not equipped
for political life.   He can, it is true, be adopted at a certain
moment by popular enthusiasm, but does not possess either
the technique or the mentality of the great statesmen and is
therefore bound to be a failure.   There would seem to be an
incompatibility between the spirit of the poet, centred on
eternal things, and the spirit of the true statesman, centred
on the infinite and powerful variations of men as they are on
earth.   In any case the adventure of literary men in France
in the nineteenth century when they intruded into the political
field seemed to point that way.   But the true lesson of the
life of Lamartine was not read properly and Romain Rolland,
Barrès, France, and many similar men, thought they could be
Lamartines of the twentieth century.   But they failed to be
even magnificent failures, and it is in the mood of disenchant-
ment that they ended their life.

   Another and more formalistic aspect of the phenomenon
must be considered closely.   It brings a strangely ineffectual
trend into the otherwise admirable development of French
art, both in prose and verse.   Never was Verlaine a truer
prophet than when he gave out this precept, which, however,
he failed to observe:

   Prends l'éloquence et tords-lui son cou.

It is a curious thing that after La Bruyère, after Voltaire, after

Stendhal, there should have been a necessity in France to 'take eloquence, and wring its neck.' It should have been done long ago in the country which had established that marvellous tradition of precision in prose which is one of the harder achievements of mankind. But eloquence is the weapon of the politician, and when Hugo and Lamartine went into politics eloquence was let loose. Two bad traditions arising out of two good things flowed into the turgid river. There was first of all that wonderful Cicero, the movement of whose periods is still heard in the House of Commons and in the Chambre des Députés. This in France had been reinforced by the powerful speeches of Vergniaud, Danton, Robespierre, etc.; the false bombast of modern times had been added to the true bombast of antiquity. The French were not alone guilty in this matter, since it is truly reported that the eloquence of Lord Chatham was of such a kind as had rarely been heard west of Constantinople (a false and over-optimistic estimate).

Unfortunately for the French writers of this classical school of nonsense, they also came into all the nonsense that arose from the wickedly bad translations of Shakespeare on which the French Romantics, who were mostly illiterate as regards modern languages, were fed. It is particularly unfair of the English to be so harsh on the misdemeanours in style of French Romantics like Hugo, when in fact it is English literature which is responsible, and the French were only trying to do their best to imitate what they thought was Shakespeare's greatness.

We might forgive the Romantics as having been naïvely taught in a bad school. But can we forgive the late nineteenth-century writers who should have known better? Rhetoric of the worst, feeblest, most antiquated kind is the bane of large quantities of Maurice Barrès, of Romain Rolland, even of Anatole France, whose irony disguises it only faintly. One of Barrès's books is actually entitled, *Du sang, de la volupté et de la mort*. Neither Lamartine nor Hugo would have dared to be so bad. That the country of

Voltaire should have produced this bombastic type of old-fashioned writing is a true source for wonder. That the country in which it had been said 'le moi est haïssable' should have produced 'le culte du moi' two and a half centuries later is unbelievable. But the matter is not so much one of ideology as one of style. Two potentially great writers, Péguy and Claudel, have been destroyed by this malady of eloquence, to which is attached the extravagant showing of *le moi*, the writer's self brought on the stage and parading up and down as in the strutting barn-door dance in *The Beggar's Opera*. Péguy is on the whole a political writer, with the exceptions which will be revealed later, in which, as in *Victor-Marie, Comte Hugo*, he is a great moralist and a great critic. But his style is made up of endless repetition and unbearable exaggeration. He is typically French in spirit, but he is so typically bad French in the mannerisms of his style that he falls out of any good French tradition, and luckily but naturally fails to create a tradition of his own. As for Claudel, he has a bombastic manner of writing that has probably never been surpassed; sometimes the power of his thought or the aptness and force of his expressions compel our unwilling admiration, but the result produced on a cultured reader is the impression of a semi-lunatic railing at day's length on matters incomprehensible to men, though there are occasionally outbursts of obscenity which help but a little. And yet something akin to greatness seems to exist somewhere in him. The direct connection between Claudel and politics is not so obvious, but it is intimate, though hidden. Claudel is essentially a reactionary Catholic in the service of the diplomacy of an anti-clerical regime. His eloquence is a semi-conscious political manœuvre trying to hide under a would-be magnificent veil. The fact is that he does not agree with his employers on a single point. The case is interesting psychologically, but from the literary point of view we can only note the destruction of thought by false, forced eloquence of the worst type.

In conclusion, it would seem that any attempt in literature

to come down into the political arena is bound to be a dismal failure; conversely, no attempt of politicians to rise into literature seems to have been of any value.   Clemenceau's *Au soir de la pensée* is particularly bad.   Perhaps Anatole France's M. Bergeret series come nearest to escaping failure, because even in his political ideas Anatole France kept a detachment and a power of irony which was lacking in Barrès, in Rolland, in Péguy, in Claudel.   But even in Anatole France's masterly hand the material hardly shapes into artistic forms, and as we forget quarrels of fifty years ago, Monsieur Bergeret must become more and more of a bore.

Our conclusion can only be a warning to the few writers who want really to be writers to leave politics strictly alone.

A NOTE ON THE THREE *affaires* THAT BECAME SUBJECTS FOR CONSIDERABLE LITERARY ACTIVITY UNDER THE THIRD REPUBLIC. (1) THE PANAMA AFFAIR; (2) THE BOULANGER ADVENTURE; (3) THE DREYFUS AFFAIR

The Panama Affair

The Suez Canal had been finished in 1869, and its creator, Ferdinand de Lesseps, was acclaimed as a man of genius. He was then sixty-four.   At Suez he had triumphed over all the technicians, and had built the canal in spite of them, achieving the impossible.   At seventy-four he launched the enterprise of cutting another canal through the Panama isthmus.   He was socialistically inclined, ignorant of finance as well as of technique, and lived by faith.   He refused to recognize the necessity for locks, appealed to the small investor for too small a capital, and was driven to buy off journalistic critics.   The yellow fever, the high ground, and corruption beat the old visionary.   The Baron Jacques de Reinach and Cornelius Herz were the great Jewish financiers of political corruption; Georges Clemenceau, later to become great in another way, was one powerful instrument.   But corruption did not avail. The great public (great in yet another way) inevitably found out what was going on, and in 1893 the judges of the republic did their best. Lesseps was eighty-eight and no longer understood: he was given five years. All the politicians were acquitted, or rather let off. Maurice Barrès, in *Leurs figures* mainly, tells the story. Anti-Semitism was launched by Édouard Drumont in his famous book, *La France juive* (1866); the part played by Jewish financiers in the Panama affair provided the movement with much popular feeling.

The Boulanger Adventure

In 1886, largely under the influence of Clemenceau, then an important leader of the Radicals, General Boulanger became minister for war. He played with both sides, giving hopes also to the Royalists, and exploited in his own interests a German provocation (a French functionary, Schnaebele, had been invited by a German functionary to cross the border, and then arrested—but the old German Emperor William I had ordered Schnaebele's release). Popular feeling accepted Boulanger as 'Le Général de la Revanche,' and he became an important political figure and a candidate to dictatorship—perhaps to an imperial throne. In January 1889, against Clemenceau, now his enemy, Boulanger was elected by Paris as deputy by a large majority. He might have seized power: he did not dare, wanting to remain within republican legality, and then lost ground rapidly. The Government decided to arraign him before the Senate, acting as a High Court of Justice. The police scared the general's mistress, who ran away to Brussels. On 1st April, All Fools' Day, the general followed her, the police winking wisely at his escape. He became thus a ridiculous figure. The general elections of September 1889 abolished the Boulangist party. The general committed suicide in the best romantic manner, after his mistress had died of consumption in 1891. Maurice Barrès tells the story in *L'Appel au soldat*.

The Dreyfus Affair

In 1894 a Jewish captain, Dreyfus, was arrested on a charge of spying on behalf of Germany, on a document on which his handwriting had been cunningly imitated. A court martial condemned him, after being shown further secret documents not shown to the defence. To the end he swore he was innocent. He was sent to the penal settlement of French Guiana.

In 1896 Colonel Picquart, a new chief of the Deuxième Bureau, a man of culture and of high integrity, then an anti-Semite and fully convinced of Dreyfus's guilt, in the course of his normal work came across a letter from the German military attaché to a French officer of Hungarian origin, Esterhazy, which proved Esterhazy to be a traitor. In investigating this case, Picquart discovered that the handwriting of the first document on which Dreyfus had been condemned was really Esterhazy's.

Picquart's chiefs were horrified: the honour of the army was at stake. An innocent man had been condemned, not only on a false charge, but illegally as well, since further documents had been hidden from the defence and every one now knew it. Picquart was disgraced and sent to Tunisia. Thus the French General Staff, through moral cowardice, in order not to admit of an error that was not in itself dishonourable, became not only accomplices, but principals, in a crime.

Picquart refused to be silenced. The Senate was appealed to. Zola published in Clemenceau's newspaper L'Aurore a letter entitled J'accuse, in which he made all the facts public. Passionate feeling was aroused at first among the intellectuals, then among the political parties of the Left who suspected the General Staff of anti-Semitic tendencies and reactionary sympathies, and at last throughout the nation.

Then, perhaps in a fit of criminal zeal, a staff officer, Colonel Henry, produced another forgery, which, if accepted, would have proved Dreyfus guilty. But by now everybody was on the alert: the forgery was exposed and Henry committed suicide. This brought to the mass of the French nation the certainty that Dreyfus was innocent; otherwise it would not have been necessary to forge documents against him.

So it was decided to try Dreyfus again in 1899. Incredibly enough, the new court-martial again condemned Dreyfus, but this time acknowledged extenuating circumstances (and the most respected judges had voted for the acquittal). How could there be extenuating circumstances to high treason? So Dreyfus was pardoned and his family accepted the pardon.

Then the *affaire Dreyfus* went mad. The French went into a two-party fury, the parties on the right (with some honourable exceptions) making Dreyfus's guilt a party dogma, the parties on the left using the popular indignation against an obvious official crime to swing themselves into power. The man Dreyfus himself was more or less forgotten. The republic thus became a Radical-Socialist republic under Combes. So in 1906 the Cour de Cassation declared the judgment of the courts martial illegal; Dreyfus was rehabilitated. Picquart was made a general and later became war minister. But a whole band of political profiteers acquired important positions. Péguy coined his great formula: 'La mystique devient une politique.' Zola and Péguy were heart and soul in the pro-Dreyfus movement. Anatole France also took a leading part in it; some of the Bergeret series, that perfect little masterpiece *Crainquebille*, and some of the most telling parts of *L'Île des pingouins* are full of the Dreyfus affair. *L'affaire* still echoes down the reverberating volumes of Marcel Proust.

ANATOLE FRANCE: 1844–1924

ANATOLE FRANCE was born as François Anatole Thibault and lived to eighty. His great-grandmother was called Françoise, his great-uncle was called François; his father was called François Noël. They were from Anjou, where the peasants shorten François into France, even as the Germans say Franz. The great novelist had therefore a right to call himself France —an otherwise unforgivable impertinence—and he made good his title to the name. He was born in Paris of a mother who belonged to Chartres. Nothing could be more French in the most intimate sense than this descent: Anjou, Chartres, Paris. No purer flower was born from the French earth. To cap it all, France's father was a bookseller—a seller of rare books—in the very centre of Paris, and most of the cultured people of Paris came to chat in his shop in the hearing of the little boy. Providence took the most precise pains to produce and then educate the future author of *La Révolte des anges*, the destroyer of Bossuet and Milton, the disciple of Bossuet and Milton.

From 1888 the central role in his private life is held by Madame de Caillavet, whose name must be honoured, since France said—and it was practically the truth, though not quite: 'Sans elle, je ne ferais pas de livres.' She drove him into the French Academy, and was great enough to know that the French Academy was only a stage to a deeper glory. She got him out of his silly enthusiasm for General Boulanger, of whom she said: 'Il me fait douter de l'histoire—je me demande si toutes les grandes figures ne sont pas faites d'un panache, d'un plumet et de l'engouement populaire.' She threw him into the battle of the Dreyfus affair, and on the right side. She introduced him to Jaurès, the greatest of the French Socialist orators. When she died in 1910, he wrote: 'Ma vie est finie.' But his work had not yet reached its summit; he was still to write his final masterpiece, *La Révolte des anges* (1913).

The war of 1914–18 killed his faith in the future of mankind as he had known it, and he ended his life a declared Communist.

Thus Anatole France began as a charming individual and ended as a formidable figure, whose true greatness is hardly seen even now. He is thoroughly at one with the period, and yet in him is the full fruit of a much longer tradition. Just as Mallarmé flowers in Valéry, Voltaire flowers in Anatole France. *Candide* culminates in *La Révolte des anges*, in which, on a much grander stage, Voltaire at last bows to Leibniz and agrees finally, through Satan's mouth, that all is for the best in the best of all possible worlds; the accent is still on *possible*. *L'Ingénu* reappears as Évariste Gamelin in *Les Dieux ont soif*; the man who looks for justice with too undivided a mind becomes all too quickly a terrorist.

But a long education was necessary before France applied his great native gifts to worthy subjects. When young, from *Le Crime de Sylvestre Bonnard* to *Le Lys rouge*, he was just a mischievous and irresponsible adolescent who could write divinely and do juggler's tricks with any idea that ever came into the human mind. Many people still find in the books of that period, in *Le Livre de mon ami*, *La Rôtisserie de la Reine Pédauque*, *Thaïs*, their greatest delight. Anatole France was a late grower: he was already thirty-seven at the date of *Le Crime de Sylvestre Bonnard*, and he never left off growing— his last books are his great ones. These early novels are already exercises in irony and pity, the two moods that took him through a long life. But they could be called superficial, for all our delight in them. He then applied his gifts to a survey of his contemporaries in a crisis of the most telling kind: the *affaire Dreyfus*. The four volumes on M. Bergeret make interesting reading rather than great reading. France is adjusting his optical instruments to events that are a little too near him. But behind irony and pity loom larger a love of justice and a love of liberty that give a more serious tone to his writing. Art is trying to come to grips with life, not quite succeeding yet. They gave France his range. It is not the *Histoire contemporaine* (1896 – 1901) that was to give him his chance, but history proper. *L'Île des pingouins* is a long sarcastic study of history; *Jeanne d'Arc* (1908) enables France to focus on a special point, but the point is unfavourable to his genius; Sainte Jeanne is the one historical character that is beyond Anatole France; then he finds his subject, the French Revolution, and produces at last his first great masterpiece (his previous successes were only small masterpieces, like *Thaïs*), *Les Dieux ont soif* (1912). Not too near, like M. Bergeret and Dreyfus, not too far, like Joan of Arc.

What were the great men of the Revolution? Danton, Robespierre, their royalist adversaries? Indeed they were small men. The fact that they killed each other so impresses us that we attribute greatness to them; but they were not great, they did not understand what was happening. Death, once started, goes on by itself. A moment comes when the terrorists' desire to kill is less strong and less quick than the victims' desire to die. A strange lust for death takes hold of all. Perfectly good republicans pretend to be royalists in order to be killed at once; many despise the guillotine as pedantic and slow, and just kill themselves. The gods are exacting blood.

A defeated general is tried for his life: 'Dans cette affaire tout était incertain, contesté; position des armées, nombre des effectifs, munitions, ordres donnés, ordres reçus, mouvements des troupes; on ne savait rien. Personne ne comprenait rien à ces opérations confuses, absurdes, sans but, qui avaient abouti à un désastre, personne; pas plus le défenseur et l'accusé lui-même que l'accusateur, les juges et le juré, et, chose étrange, personne n'avouait à autrui ni à soi-même qu'il ne comprenait pas—Gamelin, d'une voix sourde, qui s'étranglait dans sa gorge, mais d'un ton résolu, déclara l'accusé coupable de trahison envers la République et un murmure approbateur, qui s'éleva dans la foule, vint caresser sa jeune vertu.' *L'Ingénu* kills the general.

The fourteenth chapter is as good as anything in *Candide*. A former financier aristocrat who is an atheist, a Barnabite friar, and a prostitute dispute on the great truths of religion, and the illiterate prostitute proves far the best theologian. As for the former financier aristocrat, 'le sage n'était pas surpris que des êtres misérables, vains jouets des forces de la nature, se trouvassent le plus souvent dans des situations absurdes et cruelles. Mais il avait la faiblesse de croire que les révolutionnaires étaient plus méchants et plus sots que les autres hommes, en quoi il tombait dans l'idéologie; du reste, il n'était point pessimiste et ne pensait pas que la vie fut tout à fait mauvaise.'

And what of love? That is, indeed, one of the divine forces: Évariste Gamelin is, of course, beheaded with Robespierre in Thermidor. In the following Nivose, his best friend, Desmahis, takes his place with his mistress Élodie. And at the end of the book, Chapter XXIX, in the early morning, she says to him (but who is 'him'? Évariste? Desmahis?) what she had said in the early morning to the other 'him' (Chapter XI): 'Adieu, mon amour—c'est l'heure où mon père va rentrer; si tu entends du bruit dans l'escalier, monte vite à l'étage supérieur et ne descends que quand il n'y aura plus de danger qu'on te voie. Pour te faire ouvrir, frappe trois coups à la fenêtre de la concierge. Adieu, ma vie, adieu, mon âme.' An eternal speech, to be repeated for ever. A bad lot, evidently. But mankind goes on: 'Les derniers tisons brillaient dans l'être. Élodie laissa retomber sur l'oreiller sa tête heureuse et lasse.'—FIN.

But *La Révolte des anges* (1914) is the final masterpiece. Irony and pity and love of justice and liberty transcend the human plane. Can a novel, while remaining a novel and telling you tales of adultery (the proper function of the novel, really), yet rise to the epic plane and tell us at last what did happen to Satan in the end? For there was, until then, much doubt on the subject.

Milton, of course, damned Satan eternally. Marlowe damned Faust eternally. But the European mind is prone to appeasement.   Goethe forgives Faust, thereby ruining his drama as drama.   (Marlowe is a much greater poet and dramatist than Goethe.)   Now, Milton's Satan had, as all know, some regret for his action against Adam and Eve.   But he severely repressed his good tendencies.   Hugo's Satan, on the contrary, in the great French epic *La Fin de Satan* unashamedly confesses that he loves God.   Such is his eternal punishment: to love God and yet to be cast out from God's love.   Satan's hatred of God and man is only a deep repression of his love. This Satan of Hugo's is much less impressive than Milton's, but is much more touching, much more human.   He makes his own hell; his conversion will bring him to heaven.   Hugo is more human than Milton; truer too, psychologically: man's will is always done, but not in the way man plans.   Satan does re-enter heaven, but not as a conqueror; he comes back forgiven.   Thus Satan's deepest will is done, against his superficial will.   For in reality he rebelled, not to conquer (how could he conquer God?   Satan is not a fool), but to be forgiven.   He committed his crime to be forgiven of God, and thus to be sure that he was loved.   For how could he know otherwise?

That seemed indeed, about 1860, the end: 'La fin de Satan.'

Yet, Anatole France goes further.   Not that he breaks with tradition: Milton's Satan had already accused God of stupidity: 'Who overcomes by force hath overcome but half his foe.'   Force is stupid, for it needs not to think.   The vanquished has to think.

> To work in close design, by fraud or guile,
> What force effected not.

Anatole France's Satan, descended to the earth with his angels, learns thinking.   Contrary to Hugo's idea, Satan now is not forgiven: he forgives.   God has chosen the worse part, and it shall not be taken from him.   Satan has so well planned his second attempt that he is sure of victory: God has become stupid through power.   But then Satan thinks: When he is in power, will he also become stupid and cruel?   Satan's selfishness transcends itself; for selfish reasons he will abstain from victory. But he has also for God some sympathy, some gratitude even. Had not God been ferocious and silly, Satan would not have become intelligent and kind. God truly is the victim. It is Satan's kingdom that is not of this world, and that is why, by a final paradox, he reigns on earth. 'Compagnons, dit le grand archange, non. Ne conquérons pas le ciel. C'est assez de le pouvoir. La guerre engendre la guerre, et la victoire, la défaite. Dieu vaincu deviendra Satan, Satan vainqueur deviendra Dieu. Puissent les destins m'épargner ce sort épouvantable. J'aime l'enfer qui a formé mon génie; j'aime la terre où j'ai fait quelque bien, s'il est possible d'en faire en ce monde effroyable où les êtres ne subsistent que pour le meurtre. Maintenant, grâce à nous, le vieux Dieu est dépossédé de son empire terrestre et tout ce qui pense sur ce globe le dédaigne ou l'ignore. Mais qu'importe que les hommes ne soient plus soumis à Ialdabaoth si l'esprit d'Ialdabaoth est encore en eux, s'ils sont à sa ressemblance, jaloux, violents, querelleurs, cupides, ennemis des arts et de la beauté? — Quant à nous, esprits célestes, démons sublimes, nous avons détruit Ialdabaoth, notre tyran, si nous avons détruit en nous l'ignorance et la peur.'

Such is the final conclusion: thus do irony and pity come together. Much has been said of France's style. He deserves his name: France; he writes French in perfection. It is true he does not achieve the sublime any more than Voltaire does. Neither Bossuet nor Paul Valéry are in his orbit. But the ordinary cultured man is fully at home in Anatole France's perfect French—throughout the world. The whole world will have to learn French to enjoy Anatole France—and neither Bossuet nor Valéry would make the world do that. The world has already too many sublime prose writers, but France only has Anatole France. It is true he also fails to be a Balzac, but then, one Balzac was enough. One Anatole France was now necessary.

MAURICE BARRÈS: 1862–1923

BARRÈS was a Lorrainer by birth, and at first an egotist: secondarily he became a politician, deputy for Nancy from 1889. Behind the self that he at first cultivated exclusively he discovered his country, and perhaps at the end of his life he discovered mankind. He died too early at sixty-one; his *Journals* and his last books show that the wealth of his soul was as yet far from exhausted. Both his art and his thought would probably have risen higher and struck deeper had he lived to the age of Anatole France or Victor Hugo. A peculiar kind of nobility which the reader feels and respects leads Barrès pretty often into impossible situations, and his sharp intellect then opens his soul to the waters of bitterness. So, much of his work is bitter; and he was on the wrong side in many quarrels, because he wanted heroes to worship where there were no heroes. Thus his nobility led to bitterness, but his passionate love for France and the lasting elements of French culture kept a kind of deeper serenity behind his vagaries. His work has been exploited by parties who do not deserve to have him in their ranks. Perhaps he died too early because he was exhausted and wanted to escape

> D'un monde où l'action n'est pas la sœur du rêve.

He had tried to harmonize action and dreaming; he had not failed, but the world had failed him. The key to his tragedy is possibly in the fact that he could not really accept the Catholic faith, which was the basis of his life.

Of Barrès's first period, perhaps *Le Jardin de Bérénice* is the most pleasurable novel. It is not so different from Anatole France in his first period, *Le Lys rouge*, but Anatole France does it better. Yet it is so good that the reader is only too pleased to find that it can be done also by Barrès. Perhaps Barrès has remained truer to his youth than Anatole France: whereas France's *Révolte des anges* belongs to a different world from *Le Lys rouge* (in spite of some resemblances), Barrès's *Jardin sur l'Oronte* in 1922 is a return to the mentality of 1890 in both, before politics were politics.   And those readers who truly liked that kind of tale—legitimately—might maintain that Barrès after all is the true Anatole France, and that *Un Jardin sur l'Oronte* is a Francean book—a Francean masterpiece written by Barrès when France had been laid to rest.

Subtlety, a delicate romantic flavour, a true epicureanism, a detachment, a great sensitiveness to all outside impressions, a somewhat cynical abandon to all impulses from the inside—and excellent French.   Such is the early recipe, for Barrès as for France.   But one cannot help feeling—in spite of all the pleasure they give us—that they are not yet quite grown up.

Some temperaments have to go through a serious illness before they get their strength and mature.   Politics was this illness for both France and Barrès.   Why insist on the illness? I hold that the middle period books from *Les Déracinés* (1897) to *Colette Baudoche* (1909) are better left unread.   The racial ideas are crude, and indeed resemble overmuch other crude ideas that properly belong on the other side of the Rhine. No doubt the bitter satire of French political life in *Leurs Figures* is only too true, but one reads the malevolent pages with no joy, and literary pleasure is absent.   A powerful journalist is at work—and Barrès remained to the end a powerful journalist.   Those that read his daily articles against Caillaux at the end of the first world war will not forget the feelings that were aroused then.   *En regardant au fond des crevasses* was the title, and strange monsters curled appalling tentacles deep down in the crevices of the soil of France.

But what are politics?   Clemenceau is a sinister figure in Barrès's semi-historical novels of 1900; he has to be a hero for Barrès in 1918.   The fact perhaps proves that no literature can hallow politics.

Barrès's most durable book is *La Colline inspirée* (1909). It is the story of a pre-Celtic sacred hill in the Lorraine region, and of some peasant prophets who felt the old spirit rise in them in the nineteenth century.   This time all that was good in Barrès's patriotism and love of the ancient race came into full legitimate play. And there is no idealization of the brute peasant either; for the true peasant is not far above the animal, and animals also can be good or bad. But the rising of the religious spirit out of the sympathy between the peasant and the earth is a powerful impulse: both below the animal life really, and yet above the spiritual level of people who live in towns. This tremendous subject has never been dealt with on that level anywhere else, though several attempts have been made in the less successful regions of English literature, by writers like Buchan, for instance. Barrès has the genius of his subject, and genius is not too strong a word.

Barrès was ill at ease in his politics, and in the religion that had to go with his politics. Being above all intelligent, he knew only too well that the men he had to support were no better than those he had to attack. He knew very well that the religious party he had to side with was only a party; it was not even really the Catholic Church; besides which, he was not a Catholic. He was a rationalist trying to find in the past, in the earth, in the people, roots that should be strong enough to weather the storms. He was a rationalist who looked deeper than reason. All this had been hampering him in his *Énergie nationale* novels. Barrès was not really a salesman for patriotism: in his soul he was an artist. When he turned to the land and to the religious peasant, he found his full scope, and he drew a picture of a part of the true soul of France. Of course, his prophets had to be failures—what else was possible in our time, or so near it? But in the tale of their disaster he wove the description of their strength, and spread the mystic relationship of man and earth in the spiritual world. Not pretending to know what that spiritual world of the woods and fields is, or can be, being totally undogmatic, he therefore caught the true literary angle.

And yet *La Colline inspirée* is hard reading. All Barrès's virtuosity of style, all his profound knowledge of French, is needed, and yet the reader also has to collaborate and understand.   Both the writer and the reader have to do their utmost, and the subject remains all the time slightly beyond them both.   That impression of something great moving and living just beyond the phrase and the page is one of the creations of the highest literary art.   A strenuous but successful masterpiece.

And in his old age, just as though to show that he could yet relax and play, play with the acquired and dearly bought wisdom of maturity, he wrote in 1922 *Un Jardin sur l'Oronte*. A simple and wicked tale of the Crusaders, of a western lord who falls in love with an eastern lady, and how he comes to his death, and how perfect destiny is.   A strange book after all the great efforts.   But again a masterpiece: as though the dumb Middle Ages had become intelligent and bad, and had added to their effectiveness and *naïveté* the *ruse* and the viciousness supposed to belong to our later ages.   But who knows?   We have no reason to think the Middle Ages, especially in Syria, were not as wicked as we can ever hope to be, and Barrès leaves us wondering what we would have done *sur l'Oronte*.   Destiny also is a work of art, and the real writer can tell how a good story should go so that the pattern of his imaginary events somehow harmonizes with that obscure but inevitable force that we can only suppose to be the will of God chastising our wickedness by means of the deceitfulness of very fair, of unbearably fair, ladies, especially eastern ladies.

Here is a true synthesis of Barrès: *Le Jardin de Bérénice* is *sur l'Oronte*, but also the knight is obviously a *Déraciné* who should have stayed on *La Colline inspirée*, or perhaps managed to bring back his eastern lady to Lorraine.   Worse things have happened.   Thus Barrès ends on an ironical note and we are richer for it.

ROMAIN ROLLAND: 1866–1945

ROMAIN ROLLAND comes from the north-eastern outposts of the Massif Central, that impregnable citadel of prehistoric France, not so far from where Pascal was born. And there is something of Pascal in Romain Rolland. Pascal's dictum about killing, which is murder on one side of a frontier and virtue on the other side, represents Rolland's attitude about war. Pascal is perhaps the most French of all French great men, in an older and deeper sense than Voltaire or Anatole France are. They are French of the civilized plains; the mountains are the substance of France, the bones on which the flesh of the plains is laid, and those who know only the cities of the plain do not know France. In France mankind is created in the mountains and then flows down into the plains, where it effervesces for a while, brilliantly, then dies off to be replaced by new descents. Two-thirds of France live on a higher level than any ground in England. Romain Rolland comes from the north-east centre of France, where the uplands abut on the plains. An ancient pantheism of the people is the true religion of the mountaineers, and Romain Rolland strove throughout his life to make it clear: a pantheism that is always on the move towards polytheism and deism and never reaches Christianity proper. From this came Pascal: a desperate attempt to be a Christian and destroy all possible arguments against Christianity. Three hundred years later the problem for Romain Rolland is different: How is one to link up the ancient intuitions of the French with the feelings of the world at large? From *Jean Christophe* to *Vivekananda* Rolland carries on that effort.

He began as a historian, but a great woman, Malwida von Meysenbug, in Rome, claimed him for music: she had been a friend of Wagner. So he became a teacher of the history of music at the Sorbonne.

Romain Rolland is from many angles an extraordinary case

in recent French literature.. He was, first of all, a thinker in the musical field, and perhaps that is the key to all that was essentially original in his work. He was also a connoisseur and a lover of a certain type of German culture; a type which has been inadequate as far as Germany is concerned since the days of Wagner and Nietzsche.

Yet that type of German culture had been extremely popular in France, during both the Romantic period and the Symbolist period. For the Romantics it was represented by Goethe and Beethoven; for the Symbolists, whose chief organ was *La Revue wagnérienne*, Wagner, under a great misconception, was supposed to represent the same type of German. The Symbolists of the Mallarmé group were entirely mistaken about Wagner, and the similarities between the Wagnerian hero and the Nietzschean hero are now well understood. They were unperceived by the Mallarméans, for whom Wagner was only a bolder and more modern Beethoven. It is curious that the cult of the great man should be so directly connected with music.

Romain Rolland came to his maturity and to his fame in France during the early years of the twentieth century. The *Mercure de France* was popularizing Nietzsche throughout the French cultured classes. The Nietzschean hero and the Nietzschean ethics were in deep opposition to Romain Rolland's innermost feelings, which were essentially humanitarian, pantheistic, and pacifist. It was perhaps as a direct reaction against the enthusiasm of 1900 for Nietzsche that Romain Rolland was moved to write *Jean Christophe*. He had been, so far, busy mainly with the history of music, and had acquired a name and a high position in the teaching world as a musicologist. His innermost feeling was against Wagner and for Beethoven, and therefore, in literature, against Nietzsche and for Goethe. But his problem was not a problem of the past. It was a problem of 1900. Therefore he was driven by inner compulsion, not to historical work, but to fiction on contemporary themes.

Two contemporary problems claimed his deepest attention.

What sort of a great man could be expected to save the world, spiritually at least, in 1900? How could that great man, once imagined, solve the most pressing problem of the time in Europe, namely, the relationship between France and Germany? *Jean Christophe* was a magnificent attempt to solve these problems, and the war of 1914 was the practical demonstration that the problem had not been solved. It was consequently the end, in failure, of Romain Rolland's spiritual world. As the war became inevitable during the years between 1900 and 1914, Romain Rolland no doubt became acutely sensitive to this growing failure, and consequently the magnificent effort embodied in the ten volumes of *Jean Christophe* loses its efficacy as the work proceeds. Only the first three volumes, where the young German genius is described in his morning splendour, are really first-rate. They show the great man as the child of nature endowed with a profound pantheism which binds him in brotherhood to all mankind and to nature, and which makes him impatient of all constraint. He revolts against the growing formalism and militarism of the German State. But, of course, in a sense Jean Christophe's running away from Germany and coming to install himself in Paris is, in fact, a failure, since it cannot be from Paris that German militarism will be changed. It is therefore understandable that after the third volume the problem, instead of being universal and European, becomes personal. Instead of France and Germany being reconciled and united, it is Jean Christophe and a young French intellectual that become great friends.

No doubt Romain Rolland shows admirably that a 'good' German and a 'good' Frenchman can be friends. But then the whole theme is transposed into a sentimental and private plane. It is no wonder that as the ten volumes proceed the tale becomes more and more pessimistic. The advance shadows of the catastrophe obviously obliterate hope in Romain Rolland's heart. Had he been deeply sincere with himself he could have made the latter part of the book into a magnificent human tragedy. But he would not admit the failure, and closed his eyes to the realities of the situation. This lack of innermost sincerity necessarily makes the novel fall to lower levels in the literary sphere. The great novel becomes more and more diluted and ends, as some great rivers do, in a morass, where the geographer can hardly trace its course.

Some of the later volumes are, of course, deeply interesting, since both the intellect and the artistic sensitiveness of Romain Rolland are still in full action. The opposed volumes of *La Foire sur la place* and *Dans la maison* give a picture of France before the war of 1914 which is extremely illuminating. But it can be said, nevertheless, that only the first three volumes, from *L'Aube* to *La Révolte*, are in the front line of literature. The war of 1914 marked the complete failure of all this ideology. By his refusal to confess failure Romain Rolland was driven into the position described in *Au-dessus de la mêlée*. That he hated German militarism is perfectly sure. But then he hated militarism in itself, and was quite prepared to denounce it among his own people. He tried to judge the conflict in an objective manner from the point of view of the interests of mankind in general. Not unnaturally, in a period of great stress and hasty judgment, he was accused of being a pro-German, which was not true in the sense in which it was said.

Perhaps the most interesting product of this period is the play *Liluli*, which is a kind of allegory in which the rich, the poor, the fat, the thin, play parts which might have been better situated in the history of literature somewhat early in the Middle Ages, that is to say, before literature really began. Allegory of that kind can result, and in this case did result, in absolute childishness. It is perhaps impossible to read *Liluli* without a feeling of shame that so great an intellect as Romain Rolland's should obviously, through the deep sincerity of the man, allow itself to sink below the level at which literary criticism is possible. Romain Rolland was attempting to write scripture, but really did not reach even into the sphere of literature proper. In fact, it was the crudest sort of journalism put on the stage. And yet, one has to admire the moral integrity of the man, who is thus lowering his mind.

He had tried the stage in his earlier period with plays on the French Revolution. But, again, these were not really plays at all. They were sermons on the revolutionary virtues, and very obviously his presentation of Danton and the others is utterly different from reality. It can be said also that as a dramatist Romain Rolland was a complete failure. Again, his moral preoccupations prevented him from reaching artistic effectiveness.

This period made him an international leader of the pacifist movement on the spiritual plane. He was a great figure in the movement in the sense that many members came to him as to a prophet. But he could not, of course, take an effective part in it. This second period really falls within the sphere of journalistic activities rather than of literature. But it no doubt embodied a natural reaction to the failure of the *Jean Christophe* mentality.

But although the literary man had lost his power, the spiritual man had not, and the personal prestige and human influence of Romain Rolland grew even greater as he became older. His ideas and spiritual impulses, baffled on the political plane, and checked at every point by the development of European history, transferred themselves to a cosmic plane. The great man, as conceived in 1900, was insufficient. The Europeans were really untaught children. Hence Rolland's extraordinary flight to India. His contacts with Indian students, thinkers, religious leaders, and political men became close and numerous, and his volumes on Indian thinkers make extremely interesting reading of a somewhat pathetic character. Obviously he was over-anxious to persuade us and he was perhaps not entirely convinced that he was doing the right thing. It is also difficult not to feel that the old myth created beyond the Rhine of a deep resemblance between Germany and India held sway in the dark recesses of Romain Rolland's mind.

But after all this an extraordinary spiritual event took

place: at seventy-four years of age, in 1940, closed in by the war and the disaster of France in a small town in the very country he came from, and in a Catholic high place, Vézelay, Romain Rolland at last gained complete possession of his soul and of his art, and produced his true masterpiece. The great man, the hero he had been longing for all his life and never finding, had been living all the time under Rolland's eye. He was no other than his best friend, Péguy.

Now Péguy, as an artist, had never come off. But Romain Rolland, in perfect sincerity, lifted himself into the exalted position of Plato towards Socrates. He created Péguy. Out of the confused material of interminable pamphlets, and even more interminable poems left by Péguy, Romain Rolland, in the years of France's greatest humiliation, created a magnificent work of art. Péguy was a man of genius, and a great man: his works are full of illuminations of every kind: thought and phrase. So Rolland shaped a double work. First he presented the great soul of Péguy in its tumultuous course. Here was the true Jean Christophe at last, the real hero prophet, changing his mind every few years to remain true to his living soul, and dying a hero at the battle of the Marne, having known of that death and prepared for it as for his supreme triumph for several years. Then Rolland wove in, very artistically, innumerable and lengthy quotations from Péguy's prose and poetry; so that all the best of Péguy, all his true genius, is present in extracts in this masterpiece.

And here is much besides: a picture of the spiritual state of France from 1880 to 1943, since Rolland overflows his subject and brings in everything of interest during that period. Péguy has had a posthumous life and influence which lasts into the book.

But Rolland transcends Péguy; he judges him. He is not carried away; in full sympathy he yet gives true and profound judgment on Péguy's Catholicism and violent reactionary fits; Rolland remains Rolland and judges Péguy—and the French nation—from a universal point of view. And not only Péguy. Here is the best criticism yet formulated on Taine, on Renan, on Brunetière, on most others down to Malraux, down to Bernard Shaw's *Joan of Arc*, annihilated in one page.[1]

In all his other books Rolland is too long and too disorderly, but now at last he had achieved true art. He is concise and plans well. His rather turbid style has also settled down: it has kept the power it has acquired—clarity and equilibrium.

Thirty years of meditation and passion have settled into a great work: 'calm of mind, all passion spent,' all wisdom acquired. From November 1939 to November 1943 Romain Rolland triumphantly justified himself and his friend in at last a complete masterpiece, returning to a completely French theme, after his German and Indian experiments. A unique event. I cannot recall in real history a case of so late and so perfect a maturing of a great mind. No doubt the calamity of France's downfall drove Rolland's soul down to its ultimate foundations, and his book is a vindication of the deepest French spirit. Péguy and Rolland are complementary opposites, and in this artistic synthesis is a triumph of the French at the hour of their direst downfall.

[1] '. . . de l'esprit, de l'émotion; intelligente, vive et humaine—la pièce de Shaw n'a de racines en rien; elle est posée sur le vide esthetique et moral, d'un cosmopolitisme d'art "intellectuel," qui ne croit pas à la réalité intérieure de ce qu'il raconte, en l'expliquant à la façon d'un protestant instruit et sceptique—c'est à dire en niant au fond—oh! courtoisement, avec sympathie! Il pense que c'est assez de compatir aux erreurs, pleines d'un bon sens paysan, aux faiblesses de la jeune victime, pour entrer dans la vérité de son personnage. Mais il s'arrête à l'entrée. Il n'a aucune idée du monde intérieur qui remplit l'âme de Jeanne, comme de tout ce peuple qui l'entoure.'—This, by the way, also annihilates Anatole France's *Jeanne d'Arc*.

LITERARY CRITICS

THE French are supposed to be great critics. An impartial study of history does not support that view. Sainte-Beuve is in some ways a great historian in his *Port-Royal*, but he is a bad literary critic. He is always wrong—by which I mean that a cultured man of to-day cannot agree with any of Sainte-Beuve's decisions on his contemporaries. In any case no reliable critic emerged during this period, although many critics enjoyed a vogue.

Perhaps the most telling case is that of Brunetière (1849–1906), who became about 1900 a sort of literary pope. He was the master of the *Revue des Deux Mondes* and of the Académie française. Nowadays there is not a single book of his that can be recommended: anybody can read his *Balzac* and see what a poor judge Brunetière was. He invented and upheld with an obstinacy which proves either bad faith or stupidity a doctrine of the *évolution des genres*. Very strange of Brunetière, who was the main pillar of religion in the most old-fashioned sense—although a non-believer. He merely thought it was good for the State that the 'lower classes' should believe, and thus be more easily ruled. Lenin's dictum that religion is the opium of the people applies exactly to the kind of religion that Brunetière, Lemaître, Barrès, Maurras wanted to establish in France. Why then should Brunetière conceive of lyric poetry, or the drama, or the novel, as of a Darwinian species that evolves from this or that cause?

Bad books evolve because a bad writer imitates a previous good one. Hugo puts it thus:

Sur le Racine mort le Campistron pullule;

so the evolution of bad writers is into nothingness.

But Racine did not evolve from Corneille, nor Balzac from Bernardin de Saint-Pierre, nor Proust from Anatole France,

64

nor Anatole France from Balzac. The whole theory is groundless and Brunetière obviously created it because, pretending to be a Catholic, he was not. He was a scientific materialist, a bad disciple of Taine (who was bad enough himself), but his political ideas prevented him from admitting this. So he relieved his innermost self by expressing Darwinian ideas in a field in which he could do as he liked without arousing his political friends' opposition: the literary field, about which his friends cared little, but in which Darwinian ideas apply least well of all.

Thus Brunetière was divided against himself. He was the prime mover in two literary crimes that are still of importance to-day; a senseless depreciation of the eighteenth century and a senseless depreciation of Victor Hugo. In both cases the crimes had political reasons. The eighteenth century was sacrificed because of a love for autocracy, a system of which Louis XIV is supposed (falsely) to be the pattern; as for Hugo, it was not his literary faults, numerous though they are, that caused his excommunication, but his democratic feelings. Faguet, Lemaître, and Maurras followed Brunetière. There was no *évolution* in that *genre*, and they falsely deceived generations of readers, who therefore no longer even read Hugo or Diderot or Rousseau.

Literary criticism, in fact, degenerated into political journalism.

Besides, Brunetière wrote very bad French. He is the worst writer of all that series and yet he was acknowledged their absolute master.

Faguet (1847–1916) is a more ingenious mind, and can be read with some pleasure on the seventeenth century. He has managed to avoid the worst theories of Brunetière, while adopting similar judgments. But practically everything he says is false, in this way: if you read the author of whom Faguet speaks, you cannot understand how Faguet came to his conclusions. It is a possibility that he never read the authors of whom he spoke, but simply wrote about them from the sound of their names and what he remembered having heard about them at school. Léon Daudet, whose political ideas are the same as Faguet's, and who therefore cannot be suspected of partiality against him, says that Faguet is like the drunken driver of one of those water-carts that sprinkle the dusty streets in the summer, and zigzag beautifully from one side of the road to the other. Thus, says Daudet, does Faguet pour out praise and blame impartially on all comers, irrespective of their merits.

Lemaître (1853–1914) might have been a literary critic in better days. But he had to take over from Brunetière and become the great upholder of nationalism, religion, and even royalism, linking up with Charles Maurras and the *Action française*: that is, with the worst sort of political journalism, using literary criticism as a weapon. Maurras was the worst and the cleverest of that line, and the leader of the anti-Romantic campaign. But it is obvious, as Lanson has pointed out, that Maurras himself is an utter Romantic, that is, one who allows his feelings to overrule his judgment.

Rémy de Gourmont (1858–1915) gives the counterproof. An abundant and intelligent critic, he fails also for the same reason as Brunetière, although his doctrine is the opposite one. He is such a staunch democrat, or even anarchist, that he cannot see good literature when it comes from the other side. Political passion no doubt perverts literary judgment, and whether you are fanatically royalist or anarchist, Catholic or atheist, makes no difference to your incompetence as a critic. The judgment of literary values must be dissociated from ideas, even from literary theories—how much more dissociated then must it be from political or religious theories.

No doubt writers must have ideas, and critics have a right to ideas, but a critic who cannot judge of the literary values of a work irrespective of both the writer's ideas and the critic's, is simply not a literary critic at all: he is a controversialist. Thus Veuillot is an enemy of Hugo, and quite a good one, but he is not a literary critic of Hugo. An atheist who cannot see the beauty of Bossuet or the depth of Pascal, a Catholic who cannot see the beauty of Hugo or the intelli-

gence of Voltaire, are not literary critics. Rémy de Gourmont invented a good phrase: he said people spoke of association of ideas, but what we needed was dissociation of
ideas, since our associations were always wrong. But he
failed to carry out his own excellent doctrine.

Nevertheless, one can browse in the wide spaces covered
with ink by all these would-be critics, and one comes inevitably now and then on good things. This can be said
also of Péguy (1873–1914), who invented a very superior
kind of journalism in *Les Cahiers de la quinzaine*. Péguy was
a great man—perhaps a very great man—but he was not a
good writer. In fact, he could not write; he *talked* in print.
His talk is often very good, even when he talks in verse,
which he does for amazingly long periods, in a work entitled
Le Mystère de la charité de Jeanne d'Arc. No one I have ever
met has read it through, but there are very good passages.
His great fault is repetition. He will not only say the same
things, but repeat the same words over and over again, as
though he were a teacher addressing a class of half-deaf
children. Nevertheless he often hits. His intellectual honesty
is amazing, his power of expression is sometimes of the
highest order. I put him among the critics because I think
the only book of his that can be called a masterpiece is his
volume on Hugo, entitled: *Victor-Marie, Comte Hugo*. Péguy
shows the pagan natural values in Hugo in an admirable
manner. Péguy's own Christian feeling, far from hindering
him from seeing the beauty of Hugo's deep pantheism, is a
help to clear judgment. Thereby Péguy is a model to critics,
and is intellectually much higher than Brunetière or Rémy de
Gourmont or any of the others. A Catholic, he does not resent
Hugo's paganism or want to change it: he wants Hugo as a
pagan. Therefore he can rise not only to Hugo, but to
Corneille and Racine and Descartes. He says of Hugo: 'Il
avait le cœur moderne, ce qui est une deuxième façon de dire
qu'il n'en avait pas. Et il avait le génie païen.' He has
admirable remarks: on Corneille's criminals, who never really
succeed in being criminals; on Racine's Iphigénie, 'comme

sa soumission à son père a un fond de cruauté'; on Corneille being deeper than Racine: 'nos blessures, nous les souffrons dans Racine, mais nos remèdes, nous les trouvons dans Corneille'; on the vulgarity of the theologians, who have found *too many* proofs of the existence of God, and thereby made it difficult for us to believe in God; on 'le désordre organique qu'il y a dans *Phèdre*.' And Péguy brings to criticism a sense of humour that rises right into philosophy, as when he writes on Kant:

'Le kantisme a les mains propres, mais il n'a pas de mains. Agis en sorte . . . que l'action de Fouillée puisse être érigée en loi universelle . . . Et même l'action de Kant. Alors, pour commencer, il n'y aurait plus d'enfants. Ça ferait un beau commencement. Tout devient si simple dès qu'il n'y a plus d'enfants. . . .'

A good joke? also sound criticism: Kant is cut off from life; perhaps philosophy is unavoidably cut off from life. Therefore on Descartes and on Kant Péguy is mostly negative. On Hugo, on Bergson, on Corneille, on Racine, he is creative: he shows his reader beautiful things which the reader would not notice. He creates new beauty in the writers he loves. It could be said, paradoxically, that Hugo became a world master only by Péguy writing on him; and it is true that Hugo's real greatness had not been seen properly before Péguy, and that none know Hugo if they have not read Péguy's *Victor-Marie, Comte Hugo*.

Also the *Note conjointe sur Monsieur Descartes* is a Péguy masterpiece. It is really not about Descartes, but about Bergson, and chiefly about Corneille's *Polyeucte*. Never mind Péguy's methods, or his titles.

'Ses titres ont toujours quelque chose de rare,' as Molière said. But this is good.

A strange conclusion that the best critic of the Third Republic should be Péguy, who really was a poet that had failed, a Catholic on the verge of excommunication when he was killed in the battle of the Marne—just because he was a sound and subtle thinker, and an honest man.

It would be unjuſt not to mention Guſtave Lanson, the greateſt of university teachers of literature. Teaching is not criticism; yet teaching can be a noble art also. Lanson's manual, *Hiſtoire de la littérature française*, deserves to survive and to be carefully ſtudied; it has great literary qualities, and gives food for thought on every page. I know of no other manual that comes anywhere near it. The neareſt is that chapter of Voltaire at the end of *Le Siècle de Louis XIV*, on the great seventeenth-century writers. Lanson has also written a firſt-class book on Voltaire. Péguy deteſted Lanson—but liked him, really; juſt as he deteſted and liked Voltaire.

Péguy published his pamphlets, and even his poems, in *Les Cahiers de la quinzaine*, a queer enterprise that included comments on contemporary events in the grand journaliſtic manner as well as true works of literature. The *Revues* proper played a great part in the daily give-and-take of literature. To the senior enterprises of *La Revue des Deux mondes* and *La Revue de Paris* were added many of those big monthly or fortnightly publications of which each one is equivalent to a volume. *Le Mercure de France* and *La Nouvelle Revue française* played specially important parts; *Le Mercure de France* flourished down to 1910, and *La Nouvelle Revue française* took pride of place from 1910 to 1940. Rémy de Gourmont was the guiding spirit of *Le Mercure de France*, whose chief gift to French literature was perhaps the presentation of Nietzsche in the firſt years of the century; apart from that a realiſtic spirit presided in the periodical, and it continued the Zola line at the same time as the Symboliſt line for rather a long time after the two tendencies were dead in the intelleĉtual world. It is rather a judgment on Nietzsche, who was on the one hand a complete materialiſt—of a determiniſt kind—and on the other hand a Symboliſt poet of the Superman and the Eternal Return: entities that really never became concrete in the imagination. There is a kind of awful resemblance between Nietzsche and Maeterlink which pulls them both down in the énd to inescapable mediocrity, and *Le Mercure de France* was the mausoleum and not the triumphal arch for Nietzsche. Nevertheless *Le Mercure de France* was a vehicle of culture for a rationalist class in France, which at one time coincided with a certain bourgeoisie. It had a good clientele of intellectual doctors and professional men, and published bibliographies of all that appeared that are historically of great interest. But after Rémy de Gourmont's death, and the passing of the rationalist-symbolist synchronism, the *Mercure* became a stodgy institution, although it always contained things of interest. Gide then founded *La Nouvelle Revue française* in 1910, so as to prepare the ground for Proust, although he knew it not; it was an age of false starts that were to be put right. Actually Montfort, of *La Turque*, was editor of a first number of *La Nouvelle Revue française*, and was merrily going on with the Zola tradition— a useless performance, which Gide put right at once. The first number was cancelled and *La Nouvelle Revue française* headed straight for the future Proust, and then Proust in his turn overlaid Gide and left to him the rôle of administrator of an intellectual capital that had grown too big for Gide. Proust really came into his kingdom after his death, and *La Nouvelle Revue française: hommage à Marcel Proust* is probably the highest achievement of the *Revues*. Thereafter *La Nouvelle Revue française* and the publishing house of Gallimard exercised a sort of tyranny over the minds of the young that was not all to the good. It tended to become a *chapelle*, and perhaps a *combine*: an industrial house, in spite of Jean Paulhan's eclectic taste. Supervielle was one of Paulhan's discoveries and enthusiasms. Schlumberger also belonged to the house—but the firm attempted to sell many less deserving products to a public that was a little dazzled. Nevertheless, from 1920 to 1930 or so there was nothing in France, nor in the world in fact, so good as *La Nouvelle Revue française*. Thibaudet became its critic-in-chief—he also aroused much recrimination—but there was no one better, and his history of French literature in the nineteenth and twentieth centuries is a very stimulating book, although disorderly, incomplete, and erratic. Had he lived he would have matured into a much better critic than Brunetière or Faguet. He had at least a literary mind that worked in spite of his political preoccupations, whereas Faguet and Brunetière became mechanical party whips.

Politics, however, wrecked even more completely what could have been two great critics in Léon Daudet and Charles Maurras. In their paper, *L'Action française*, appeared occasionally some most brilliant pieces of criticism written in remarkably forcible French. But their political theories condemned them to *parti pris* of the worst kind. Daudet published a volume entitled *Le Stupide XIXᵉ Siècle*, in which he refuses to see any good in that most rich and enchanting period. To him neither Hugo nor Anatole France can be acceptable—but then he sometimes rather charmingly repented, and endorsed Gide's famous answer to the question, 'Quel est le plus grand poète français?'—'Victor Hugo, hélas.' Léon Daudet's *Mémoires* are very good in their first half; as soon as he reaches the age of politics he becomes stupid, dull, and ill-natured. Similarly, Maurras's denunciation of the Romantics as the source of all evil does not belong to literary criticism, but to the fine art of slander.

The daily press thus also had its literary critics, and Paul Souday, in *Le Temps*, stoutly upheld a solid rational and even rationalist tradition. *Le Figaro* was also a literary power in its way. But in a broader zone commercial criticism set in as a blight on much literature. Advertisement and criticism became interchangeable. Many novelists could live only by newspaper work and became critics. They had then to praise either fellow novelist-critics, or the publications of all firms that advertised in their newspapers, and the industrialization of criticism went hand in hand with that of the novel. To make a living a professional literary man had to be a journalist, a critic, and a novelist—that is to say, he had to give up his soul.

Perhaps it is better to proceed no further in this description.

CYRANO DE BERGERAC (1897)—THE DOWNFALL OF THE THEATRE

THE theatre is a great mystery. Aeschylus, Sophocles, Euripides, Aristophanes were all within one century. Shakespeare and his inferiors took less than that; Corneille, Molière, Racine encompassed only some sixty years. Then no more great dramatists in any of the three lines.

Congreve is a sort of afterthought—Sheridan is a weak dramatist—Shelley and Browning are literary reminiscences; and then? Who can say that the Irish drama is at that level?

There is no true drama after Shakespeare in England, or after Racine in France. None in Europe really. Goethe is a grand attempt, but a great failure: *Faust* is nothing as a drama compared with Marlowe; *Iphigenie auf Tauris* cannot compare with Racine. Ibsen is a freak mostly outside literature, built on 'ideas' of the weakest sort: that women should be free—and that sort of thing; that is not drama. Can you write a drama on 'that grass should be green'?

Drama demands: a great writer; a great public; a great moment. The Elizabethans plus Shakespeare plus the birth of England; Molière plus the court of Versailles and the town of Paris and the grandiose attempt by Louis XIV to master Europe; Sophocles and the Athenians and the Persian wars. A century later it is all gone. You have the seventeenth-century war on the theatre in England; the infamous century of Louis XV in France; the downfall of the free cities in Greece. A certain kind of public heroism is necessary to great drama. The great dramatist has to have his thousands ready at one spot to hear him, and on the same evenings— and he writes for them. They must somehow be on his level. Now to have the three conditions, great writer, great public, great moment together, is so difficult that in one civilization it is already a miracle if it happens once; it has, so far, never happened twice. In many civilizations or nations it has never happened at all.

Yet of course writers go on attempting plays, attracted by the glory of the past, not realizing the conditions. A novelist can send out his novel to pick out his thousands of readers one by one all over the world; so can a poet. But a dramatist writes, unconsciously or consciously—else he is no dramatist, but merely a poet or a novelist that uses dialogue—for a certain thousand that can meet one evening. If that public does not exist, cannot be gathered together physically, there is no drama. Both Shakespeare and Molière, the only two absolute successes, were actors.

Yet as no rule is absolute not only writers construct plays, but some plays get themselves written. Molière's valets come to life again at the end of the eighteenth century and strut on the stage as Figaro, the greatest of them. But Beaumarchais? Read *La Mère coupable*, the end of the Figaro series: a most lamentable performance. It is Figaro, a grandson of Molière, that created Beaumarchais.

In a similar way Rostand does not exist. But Victor Hugo's Don César de Bazan, wishing to become the central character of a play—just as Molière's valets had done with Figaro—becomes Cyrano de Bergerac, and makes Rostand write the play.

Rostand's other plays are great failures: *L'Aiglon* is a pathetic throw-back to Napoleon worship; *Chantecler* is unbearably pretentious; Cyrano lives. It is generally said that Rostand is a late Romantic. It is true, but only in a way. Cyrano is original not so much as romantic, but as sarcastic, and thus is a revelation. The Romantics in their soberer moments did not believe in Romanticism. Hugo asked to have *Les Chansons des rues et des bois* (his most unromantic production) put into his tomb as his favourite book; Musset wrote against the Romantics; Vigny despised them; Chateaubriand and Lamartine gave them up in despair; Théophile Gautier abandoned them for a nobler course. Byron wrote *Don Juan*. Masses of unpublished poems of the cynical kind remain from the Romantic poets; Musset begins a fierce poem thus, on a dance in 1830 or thereabouts:

> Quand Madame Waldor à Paul Fouché s'accroche,
> Montrant le tartre de ses dents —

In a more humane mood Hugo put into his bad drama *Ruy Blas* a sarcastic but good-humoured act about Don César de Bazan, a kindly satire of Romanticism based yet on true romantic feeling.

Rostand's Cyrano is a Romantic character afflicted with an extra large nose. Yet he is truly romantic; yet he has to be a sarcastic observer of himself and of human nature, like Don César. His central tirade on his own nose is the pivot—the nasal pivot of the play. To keep his nose up he has to be a real poet and a great soldier and a lover of a most exalted kind; again all traits of Don César.

He is a true Romantic poet. Romanticism has done no better anywhere than the song of the flute in the camp, celebrating

> — Ces airs du pays au doux rythme enchanteur
> Dont chaque note est comme une petite sœur
> — Ces airs dont la lenteur est celle des fumées
> Que le hameau natal exhale de ses toits —
> C'est la verte douceur des soirs sous la Dordogne.
> Écoutez, les Gascons, c'est toute la Gascogne —

The absurd position of the poet serenading his beloved on behalf of his good-looking but dumb friend is worthy of a Molière turned sentimental for a while—and there was much sentiment in Molière. The last act, the end of Cyrano, in 'calm of mind, all passion spent,' with the crowning recognition from the beloved when all is too late, is the acme of Romanticism, and makes good Musset's too concise boast: 'Nous rend doux et cher les chagrins passés,' or his other half-truth: 'Un sourveni "malheureux"[1] est peut-être sur terre plus vrai que le bonheur.'

[1] Musset really wrote:
> 'Un souvenir heureux est peut-être sur terre
> Plus vrai que le bonheur,'
but Cyrano's souvenirs are not exactly *heureux*—and yet they are: a perfect tragical comedy.

Cyrano is a counterpart to the Cid.   Great French drama began with tragedy that ended well, and, so far, pauses on a comedy that ends tragically.

But what a list of once glorious dead surround Rostand! It has been said that the failures of French literature would be enough to equip several nations with quite a creditable record in letters.   (Not England, however; but, say, even Ireland in the drama.)

The dreariness of Henri Bęcque (*Les Corbeaux*, *La Parisienne*) does not prevent the serious-minded from admiring him, and he is even occasionally revived.   François de Curel, Hervieu, Brieux, Mirbeau, Bataille, Bernstein, Porto-Riche (once called 'le Racine juif') are now mere names, which soon will be forgotten.   Lavedan, Donnay, Capus, Courteline, Tristan Bernard, even Jules Renard, cannot fare much better, once their realism and their humour—very transient both—have evaporated.   They really fall outside literary interests and should be studied as a sociological phenomenon.   The desire to make money in the théatre (a great temptation to any one who can write at all); the desire of the public to be amused by looking at itself (made to appear worse than it is) on the stage; and the necessity to occupy empty hours—those three elements replace the three heroic necessities.   The great author, the great public, the great moment now become the clever author, the dirty-minded public, the all-too-long moments.

Yet there is more to it than that—there always is.   There is Maeterlinck, there is Claudel, there is Giraudoux, there is Romain Rolland.   (Note: poets who try the drama.)   *Pelléas et Mélisande* hardly supports its music, and does not support its philosophy.   Maeterlinck's *Trésor des humbles* gave an impression of depth.   But one cannot be deep on the stage— the stage is a place where one must be effective.   They used to call Maeterlinck the Belgian Shakespeare in the days of *L'Oiseau bleu*.   Perhaps it is best to leave it at that.

Claudel began with an epic drama: *Tête d'or*.   No one ever discovered what it was about.   Unfortunately that applies to Claudel's best efforts in this line: *L'Annonce fait à Marie* and *L'Ôtage*. Those give opportunities to good actors, but the public goes home, even as the reader goes to bed, not knowing what he has been told, yet feeling it is of course his fault.

Le Soulier de satin has some good comic scenes. Unfortunately one does not feel sure always that Claudel meant them to be comic.

Romain Rolland tried to show how great the French revolution was, but probably the films would have been a better medium for the demonstration. The stage is not big enough for revolutions, unless an Aeschylus is the showman.

Giraudoux put on the stage a new form of fantasy, a more delicate and fanciful kind of Christmas pantomime: *Intermezzo*, *Amphitryon 38* can be seen with pleasure. *La Guerre de Troie n'aura pas lieu* was a good title, but its promises were not kept, either in the literary or in the political field.

So many other good minds registered failure in the theatre: Cocteau, Gide, Valéry even, wrote to be acted, very occasionally; Jean Richard Bloch, Supervielle also tried. It feels as though a tempting prey were apparently left unguarded, and any one going by could reach out for it. But really the fairies are watching. An invisible wall is reared between the writer and the dead beauties of ancient plays, and none gets through. On the opposite side, as specialists of the theatre, Lenormand and Obey have acquired and deserve a reputation.

Often the author becomes caught in invisible coils, and is seen no more except as a slave to the *metteur en scène*. We have had periods of great producers, showing us great actors: Gaston Baty, Pitoëf? How lamentable that the man who arranges the scenery should have become more important than the man who writes the play. Sad shades of Shakespeare and of Molière—Fernand Gregh has written three lines that are a judgment on this as on many other branches of art:

> L'Art se ressent déjà des barbares tout proches.
> Leurs idoles, que taille un coutelas grossier
> Se donnent en modèles aux maîtres sans reproche.

The *barbares tout proches* can be no other than the Germans. This supremacy of the *mise en scène* over the drama is an invention of the Germans, who have produced no drama of any real value, but who can build scenery of a peculiar nature with a *coutelas grossier*.   Reinhardt and the Berlin theatre are at the origin of this deception.   Shakespeare and Molière went about their business exactly in the opposite manner: if you have good drama the scenery is irrelevant.   Even the acting can be bad, as it must often have been in Shakespeare's plays or Racine's tragedies.   First things first.

THE TURN OF THE CENTURY

CHESTERTON stated that there is no *Zeitgeist*, that a mere section of time cannot have a spirit. But perhaps a spirit can inhabit a section of time and then go elsewhere. The facts are that centuries do differ from each other, and that within each there is a similar spirit—in some ways, not in all—and also something survives from one century to another.

This is obvious and simple as regards our earlier centuries. Ronsard died in 1585. Between him and Malherbe, whose first important work is in 1600, there is a gap and a change of spirit. Bossuet died in 1704; Montesquieu began in 1721. There is no important work between the two—but what a change in the spirit! Both Voltaire and Rousseau died in 1778, and until Lamartine's meditations in 1820 there is, in fact, nothing except bad Chateaubriand (the good Chateaubriand did not appear until 1848: the *Mémoires*). The cut and change of spirit are clear from the sixteenth to the seventeenth, the seventeenth to the eighteenth, the eighteenth to the nineteenth century. What about the nineteenth to the twentieth?

There is no gap. Good works appeared uninterruptedly from Mallarmé to Valéry. Is there a change of spirit?

Romain Rolland is nearer in spirit to Lamartine and Hugo than to Gide and Proust, his contemporaries. He is nineteenth century. What of Mallarmé and Valéry? The same ideas, the same technique, but a very different colour, and such a difference in the success. Mallarmé did not reach the public in the nineteenth century, Valéry did in the twentieth. The times are different. There is much overlapping, but the differences are easy to feel. Anatole France, Barrès: nineteenth century; in colour a blend of Hugo and Stendhal. Montherlant, Giorno: pure twentieth century. Loti, Claudel: nineteenth. Hamp: nineteenth. Jean Richard Bloch: twentieth. Jules Romains, Duhamel: begin as nineteenth but their important work is all in the twentieth. And so on. What is the difference? Psycho-analysis and the Proust mentality. None of that in France or Barrès, although actually they lived on after Proust.

The conception of a moral law has disappeared. Mallarmé and Baudelaire rebelled against the moral law because there was one.

'Une négresse par le désir secouée,' sang Mallarmé. *Les Fleurs du mal*—there was a *mal*, and you looked for it; the thrill was to break the law.

For Gide, Proust, Valéry, Malraux, Montherlant there is no law. There is no thrill in breaking the law. It has become much more difficult to find a thrill. Whether you break a social law in the search for pleasure is irrelevant. Really there is no law. It is relevant to note that the concept of law fell out of science at about the same time, to be replaced by much vaguer ideas about averages, and great numbers, and intra-atomic physics, and Brown's principle, and Einstein, and Broglie. The human mind gave a jump from the middle distance into either the infinitely small or the infinitely large, intra-atomic or past galactic, where, in either direction, the old laws no longer applied. So with Proust, who studies the infinitely small in the soul, not the self. A middle-distance delusion.

Le moi also has disappeared. *Le Culte du moi* of Barrès's early work no longer means anything. There is no *moi*. Proust's Marcel does not know what his *moi* is—and does not care.

Perhaps *le moi* was connected with the law, formed itself, as in Corneille, in submitting to the law, or, as in Baudelaire, in rebelling against it. But now, no law and no *moi*.

A curious consequence: politics fall out of literature. Barrès and France and Péguy devoted much of their time to politics. The whole series of *Les Déracinés*, that of M. Bergeret, are politics, and suffer from it. Proust, Gide, and Valéry do not bring politics into their work at all. Gide was tempted and went to the U.S.S.R.—became badly

disenchanted and said so. Would a mere matter of truth
have stopped Barrès had he decided to become a Communist?
Perhaps, however, the law is also connected with liberty.

The twentieth century, the age of no law, is also the age
of dictators and world wars.

The first true unmistakable sign is Gide's *L'Immoraliste* in
1902. The title was good. The book was an attempt, like
Chateaubriand's *René* in 1805—a portent of much to come.
Gide comes out as the Chateaubriand of the twentieth century.
He began before the others; he lived after them. He attempted
many works of art with only, really, a *succès d'estime*. He
had a tremendous influence over the young generation, very
little on the elder, who were rather shocked at him; and
finally he vindicated himself fully, after everybody—including
himself—was dead, by publishing souvenirs. Who is this?
Gide or Chateaubriand? It applies to both. Chateaubriand's
Mémoires d'outre-tombe are his masterpiece; Gide's *Journal* is
not out yet, except in fragments, but the 'modern' period,
Gidian, Proustian, is over, and the fragments we know of
Gide's *Journal* are the best of his writing. The similarity
with Chateaubriand extends to that detail: that fragments only
of Chateaubriand's *Mémoires* were known first, during his
lifetime.

It is amusing to toy with the idea: *L'Immoraliste* is another
René, the definition of a new mentality; *La Symphonie pastorale*
is *Le Dernier des Abencérages*, the attempt to assess an old
mentality; *Les Faux-monnayeurs* is *Les Martyrs*, a tale of
humbug, and, after much celebrity, a failure as *the* masterpiece;
Voyage au Tchad is *L'Itinéraire de Paris à Jérusalem*, and *Journal*
is *Mémoires d'outre-tombe*. Had Chateaubriand been reincar-
nated into the twentieth century he would have behaved
much as André Gide has behaved. He would even have
gone to Russia as well as to the Tchad. And he would have
been sick of women and love and *le moi*, even as André Gide
is, at the end.

THE ESSAY

EVERY century or so France has produced a great essayist or two, beginning with the greatest of all essayists, Montaigne, then going on to Pascal and La Bruyère, then to Vauvenargues, and one was overdue for the nineteenth or the twentieth century.

The Third Republic has had her essayist, Alain.

He began, appropriately enough, by writing for a provincial daily paper, *La Dépêche de Rouen,* as a spokesman for the Radical-Socialist party. The Paris press is not really French: perhaps—only perhaps—Parisian, but not French. The spirit and the mind of the French people are mirrored in the provincial newspaper, and *La Dépêche de Toulouse,* for several generations under the republic, has been the typically French newspaper, both Clemenceau and Jaurès being among its contributors for many years. A great essayist in *La Dépêche de Rouen* is therefore in order.

Alain is a French provincial who came to Paris. It is even tempting to see in his essays the answers to Pascal, who wrote *Lettres à un Provincial*; not so much to the pamphlet against the Jesuits, for on the Jesuits Alain heartily agrees with Pascal, but answers to *Les Pensées* themselves. What do the people, in 1900, think of Pascal's *Pensées*? What do they think on the subjects on which Pascal wrote in his defence of Christian beliefs?

Alain can speak for the people—he is of the people. He goes so far as to justify by his own case the slightly (?) corrupt practice of letting members of Parliament interfere everywhere. Had not his local M.P. used influence to get a scholarship for the boy Alain, on the recommendation of a small local teacher, Alain could not have become a teacher of philosophy. In this human world some good things are done in a slightly (?) irregular way.

Alain is the enemy of the powers that be, whatever they

be. In this really he agrees with Pascal. In his *Doctrine radicale* he explains, in his one-page essays, that as La Fontaine put it long ago,

Notre ennemi, c'est notre maître.

The prime and everlasting duty of the citizen is to resist the central power. Unless the citizen resists, the central power always becomes a tyranny, whether you have a king by divine right or a Prime Minister elected by Parliament. Power is in itself evil and corrupts all men who wield it: that is the ultimate lesson of moral psychology. But the ordinary man can watch this and stop it.

As for religion, the people's answer to Pascal runs much on the same lines: we shall believe whatever we want to believe, regardless of what the churches say. Reason is no doubt an insufficient guide, but the churches, whatever churches there be, are much worse. *Entretiens au bord de la Mer* goes as far as it can in deference to the Pascal mentality; not very far. God may be, but on condition that He remain totally helpless; He has to be helped by man at every point. That is the lesson of the Christ on the cross. Let not God presume to become absolute: then man destroys Him. Such is radical theology.

But Alain's masterpiece is no doubt *Mars, ou la Guerre jugée.* What do the people think of war? Here again Pascal is not far away: put a man in uniform, and murder becomes his duty—does murder become holy? Please note that Alain hardly mentions Pascal. But in Alain the soul of the people in 1900 answers the arrogant Puritan of 1630—and often agrees with him—but at times refutes him with violence. On war Pascal and the people agree. What is wrong about war is not so much killing those other men opposite—they are mortal and doomed, even as we are, in any case. What is wrong is that, in order to go to war, human beings have to surrender their free will into the hands of men who think only in terms of absolute authority. That is death to human nature as such, since freedom is the living breath of the soul.

In *Les Idées et les âges* Alain relaxes and rambles, which is the real function of the essayist. He goes for walks in human nature, even as Hazlitt or Dr. Johnson went for walks or drives in nature external, and reports and comments on what he sees, as Montaigne or Vauvenargues.

Alain has, however, a very terrible fault: the fault of the essayist—he never stops. Just as Montaigne never stops. His daily paper taught him to write only a one-page essay at a time; but then, it taught him to write one every day. Three hundred essays every year for forty years—or is it fifty? One volume of essays a year. Shall we pray to merciful death? Let us hope, rather, that some gifted critic in a future generation will give us an anthology of all Alain's first-rate essays, and reject into oblivion all the mediocre ones. Good hunting to all readers. To many the best and least controversial essay of Alain will be *Souvenirs concernant Jules Lagneau*, in which an extraordinary master of wisdom is described at length. Jules Lagneau, an unobtrusive yet powerful thinker, re-established the idea of God in French philosophy. More than Mallarmé himself (since Mallarmé had his own share of showing off) Lagneau was a good living example of Valéry's *Monsieur Teste*. Nowhere is Alain so human and so convincing as in the Lagneau *Souvenirs*.

Providence, who can balance its gifts, having made a present of Alain to the people of the Left, made a rich present to the Catholics in Henri Bremond. His *Histoire littéraire du sentiment religieux en France* is really an essay built on the innumerable essays written by French mystics, chiefly in the seventeenth century. Whereas Alain answers Pascal in 1900 Bremond proves, in many thick volumes, that Pascal was only one of an army of mystics in his own time and country. Bremond's work puts a new complexion on the age of Louis XIV. The French were not only the troublesome and quarrelsome *mousquetaires* that fought Europe, and on the whole won, since they took and kept Alsace, in spite of Marlborough and Prince Eugene—they were also Saint Vincent de Paul and Cardinal Bérulle. What a century! Bremond adds to the greatness of the *siècle de Louis XIV*:

perhaps he reveals its true greatness.¹ Behind the absurdities of the magnificent monarch—a Spanish monarch really, by his mother (not a truly French one): the French of Henry IV and Louis XIII, great kings both, were simple—Bremond reveals the zeal of divine love burning in the chosen—and very many were chosen. It is good that one stylist of genius, Pascal, transmitted to the following centuries something of that ardour; but innumerable truly humble mystics—Pascal was not truly humble, what writer is?—were the rank and file behind the brilliancy that sometimes betrayed them; betrayed their existence to the vain world, and also betrayed them by giving a rather false picture of them—the two kinds of betrayal go together. Bremond has now put the matter right, and it is a delight to lose oneself in his huge tomes. They are a counter-poison to Saint-Simon's huge tomes— behind and below the court and the intrigues a vast religious life was then going on all the time. Perhaps the futility of the splendour was based on the solid feeling of innumerable great souls. The real work was not of this world, but this world caught a sort of reflected glamour from the far-off effulgence of truth.

Maritain should be also praised; but truly he belongs to the philosophers and the historians rather than to literature proper; and Julien Benda, on the opposite political or religious side, belongs rather to the controversialist and journalistic side. Maritain's *Art et scolastique* is a classic of erudition and subtlety, rather too heavy, however, for us. As for Benda, perhaps he is best remembered not for his unjustified attacks on Bergson or his specious *Trahison des clercs*, but by his witticisms, as when he described Maurras greeting the victorious soldiers of 1918 by the un-Napoleonic remark:

Soldats, je suis content de moi!

Voltaire is not quite dead yet.

I⊤ is perhaps a remarkable fact that in literature there are few normal men among the celebrities. No one would call Proust normal, or Gide a specimen of the average Frenchman, or Paul Valéry a man who thinks as people in France usually do. If we go back and cogitate about Verlaine, we feel thankful that France was not made up of dumb Verlaines —or of over-loquacious but incomprehensible Mallarmés; a nation of Zolas, or even of Anatole Frances, would be rather appalling—and we need labour the point no further.

Yet we feel Molière was, in that sense, an ordinary, a normal, man. Probably Montaigne also—not so many others. Further, we rather resent the abnormality of, for instance, Proust. We resist him; we rebel against some of his finest things; we feel and say *this is not us*. Do we not refuse Baudelaire when he writes :-

Hypocrite lecteur, mon semblable, mon frère?

'Insensé, qui crois que je ne suis pas toi,' says Hugo; but we protest—we do not agree with him. We call him 'insensé' when he writes *Ce que dit la bouche d'ombre* in those *Contemplations* which he prefaces with such a sentence.

Duhamel in our time occupies this rare, and, in our time, this perhaps unique position: he is a great writer whose feelings, whose judgment, are normal, are acceptable to the ordinary cultured man. This faculty of judging as the normal man judges is exercised at its most enjoyable strength in the *Salavin* series. As a literary creation of one single character there is probably nothing to rival *Salavin* since Balzac. Salavin is far more elaborate than anything Flaubert created, and yet he has something of a mystic Madame Bovary about him. Emma Bovary was a true romantic woman who failed to make good—and yet, did she fail? Perhaps not. Similarly Salavin is a mediocre 'fellow' who tries to be a kind of mystic in a very grubby way, and who fails—and yet, does he fail?

Even as Emma Bovary's death transcends her faltering efforts in life, *Tel qu'en lui-même*, the tale of the end of Salavin, leaves the reader deeply moved.   Somehow Salavin had transcended himself.   More elaborate than Flaubert's characters, Salavin is yet a character, whereas Proust's personages cease being characters: they dissolve into concatenations of moments, and the chain may break at any point, and leave us with several Marcels, not one.   Not so Salavin: he is most formidably Salavin from beginning to end, and we shall always know him wherever he is met.

This achievement of creating one extraordinary character, who is thoroughly alive yet quite different from its author, is very rare in our period.   Proust's and Gide's characters are only fragments of their inventors.   Salavin is only Duhamel in so far as Emma Bovary was Flaubert.   Salavin, the semi-crazy mystic, is seen and judged by Duhamel as we, the readers, judge him; even as Flaubert judged Emma— with some sympathy no doubt, but with some loathing also. We understand Salavin, and Duhamel understands Salavin, not because we are Salavin, but because we, as ordinary men, are thoroughly informed about him by his author who shares our point of view.   Never perhaps in literature is this *tour de force* performed again; the character analysis is of the same order as in *La Cousine Bette* or *Le Père Goriot*, although, of course, the canvas is much smaller and can contain really only one character with a few shadows that are, however, quite alive.   Balzac was the master and the judge of his characters as no one else has been since.   Here is the nearest. In *La Chronique des Pasquier* the canvas is large, the number of characters truly delineated is large, and the life of France before the first world war well described as mirrored in the life of a family of the lower middle class, with intellectuals and business men coming out of it.   Another semi-mystic apparition, Cécile, gives just a touch of a higher life to a rather humdrum series of adventures, for many of which a French Micawber is responsible.   The father of the family is a great proof of the resilience of the human race.

More informative as to French life, and more varied and amusing than the Salavin series, the Pasquier series does not go so deeply into the realities of one character, and among the many enterprises of Georges Duhamel, the Salavin novels will probably hold the highest place.

Yet Duhamel has an extraordinary range. His books on children are perhaps his most pleasant books, and who knows but his *Fables de mon jardin* may outstrip the rest in popularity? *La Vie des martyrs* was the first book that made him famous: it may also be the most lasting of his books. These impressions and stories of a doctor that worked just behind the front in the 1914 war are most deeply disturbing in their humanity. They convey the feeling that a certain intensity of suffering is unfair to human creatures, and yet that there are human beings, and in great numbers, that are so heroic as to retain possession of their soul even in the utmost agony. A higher idea of human nature is driven into the reader by those well-nigh unbearable stories. Let us remember only that wounded young peasant who did not dare to die while his mother's eye was upon him, and had to take advantage of the physical exhaustion of the watchful woman to leave the world exactly during the two minutes when her eyes closed in spite of herself. Only Duhamel could have told that story so simply, so unavoidably. Even Balzac would have chuckled audibly and pointed out to the reader what a good story it makes. Not Duhamel. He suffers too deeply himself with the young peasant and with the old woman. He is not an author—he is a man like ourselves looking on at the acme of man's suffering.

As a stylist he is therefore an unpretentious writer. He uses the French language that all use and his art lies in the perfect adequacy of his expression to his subject-matter. He looks for no special stylistic effects; he is just natural—which is the most difficult of all things to be.

JULES ROMAINS: *b.* 1885

JULES ROMAINS is primarily a poet, but he has made his most comprehensive effort in the novel, though the dramatic form (not perhaps the drama) is familiar to him and he can be very successful in it. He belonged in his early years to a group of young poets known as 'le groupe de l'Abbaye,' with Duhamel, Chennevière, Vildrac, which has been more or less described by Duhamel in one of the Pasquier novels. They were poets who all (more or less also) found that poetry was not a career, even those that stayed in it. Duhamel found his true path with *La Vie des martyrs* in the novel; Jules Romains tried everything and succeeded (again more or less) in everything. Essentially he was a poet, an eccentric who should have starved in a garret in the ancient way. His true poems are *L'Ode génoise* and *L'Homme blanc*, and transcend his theories of *Unanimisme* (a rather fashionable idea of the sociological type—really quite feeble) and his attempt (with Chennevière) at a system of metrics. Romains has a tendency to industrialize himself that is too noticeable, and prevents a fastidious reader from doing him justice. By a kind of counter-attack his best things have hardly been noticed at all. *L'Homme blanc* would have made any other poet's fortune. It is simple in theme, subtle in treatment, forcible in expression, and, as a whole, one of the best poems of the century. Effects of rhythm and alliteration are used in a way that should have given a new direction to poetry in other times, but in our time no poet that thinks himself a poet would consent to follow any one else's lead. Lines like

> Restitue à la race royale
> Le palais partagé de ton corps

give an important place to accent in French poetry, and should point to a development and a renewal of French technique. It is widely felt that the old type of French couplet, based on

a mere count of syllables and on rhyme, has became an antiquated instrument, however brilliantly it may still be used;
every poet is trying to invent another instrument. The open
introduction of accent into French verse may well prove
fruitful. In fact, accent has always counted, from the Pléiade,
even through Racine, onwards; but it has been treated merely
as an adjunct to number of syllables. The relationship may
yet be reversed, and Jules Romains's *L'Homme blanc* counts
as one of the first of a new kind of poems.[1]

Romains's poetic gift is at the bottom of all that is successful in his immense production, but it is obscured and may
be unnoticed under the mass of his writing. In the novel
his truly amazing effort in *Les Hommes de bonne volonté*, a series
of twenty-seven volumes, relegates to the second rank, as
far as quantity in one novel goes, even Balzac himself, who
does not connect his pieces so well, or Zola, whose artificiality
in construction is too obvious nowadays. Yet in Jules
Romains's series the really great thing is the description of the
battle of Verdun in two volumes which are truly an epic presentation of war. The description of the superhuman silence
that descended on the front before the world crashed in the
great German attack will have a permanent place in literature:
it is an achievement of imagination rendered possible by the
absence of the writer from the field of battle, which permits
the deployment into genius of his capacity for being there in the
spirit. Two or three volumes on Quinette raise the detective
novel to a height which perhaps that kind of writing does not
deserve, and enrich it by the annexation of Gide's *crime
gratuit*. The description of the mentality and intrigues of professional literary men rivals *Les Illusions perdues* of Balzac (not
the best Balzac, it is true). Every type of reader will find
something in this extraordinary series. But perhaps most
readers will be left with the hope that this sort of thing will
not happen again.

[1] A young poet, Georges Lafourcade, killed accidentally during this war,
had fought a hard fight to introduce accent into French verse. He was a
devotee of Swinburne, and tried to bring English verse practices into French,
with very remarkable success. But he died too early.

It is also a whimsical kind of poetic gift which gives true value to some of Jules Romains's plays: *Monsieur le Trouhadec* is quite unforgettable and *Dr. Knock ou le Triomphe de la médecine* is a universal favourite. They are not really dramas, any more than *Le Dictateur* or any of the others, but they perhaps compare best with G. B. Shaw's so-called 'plays.' They are most ingenious, most amusing, but do not quite get rid of the quality of futility which is a by-product of the poetic mentality when used in lower *genres*.

But in all his exercises there is a queer inhuman quality in Jules Romains. Perhaps, again, this is a necessary element in all great poetry. Shakespeare is divinely indifferent to what happens to his characters, so he can wring our hearts like a malevolent god or enchant us with tales of a kind of love that is not for us. But Jules Romains, by putting this into prose, often loses contact with reality without soaring into the divine regions. Indeed he is apt to gravitate into a rather shoddy kind of infernal regions, as in some disquieting volumes of *Les Hommes de bonne volonté*. It is difficult to see how the Church of Rome can forgive Jules Romains his inventions about the private life of certain priests, and those that love France will live in hopes that some other volumes on seamy aspects of life in various classes, high and low, may not really picture the truth of facts. Some perspective has gone wrong. The poet has, for a time, a broken wing, and there is mud below.

Yet he is a poet and always soars up again, and in his immense production seekers for treasure will be immensely rewarded.

GIDE: *b.* 1869

THE masterpiece of André Gide was to be *Les Faux-monnayeurs* (1926), his only *roman*, the only work he puts before the public as a finished work of art. But André Gide has overreached himself. Thibaudet gives a definition of the failure as being 'singulièrement intelligent, mais presque exclusivement intelligent.' In fact, the book is unreadable. It marked, queerly enough, the climax of the Proust period—after Proust's death —and immediately afterwards the collapse of the Proust mentality. The younger men, Montherlant, Chamson, Malraux, repudiate as a vile insult the idea that they are *faux-monnayeurs*. They want to create new values, but clean ones; they do not want to counterfeit the old one.

Gide himself implicitly admitted his failure by publishing soon after *Le Journal des faux-monnayeurs*. Since the book was unsatisfactory perhaps a detailed story of the writing of the book could be made into a success. But it was not. It needed double-dyed Gidian fanaticism to swallow that bait. It is interesting to mark that about 1927–30 such fanaticism did exist among the younger people. It is even more interesting to note that it died soon after.

It is said of Condé that before the battle of the Dunes he took a young foreign officer out of his camp to see his adversary Turenne's dispositions and he asked the young man: 'Have you yet seen a battle?' 'No,' said the young officer. 'Well,' Condé went on, 'to-morrow you will see how a battle is lost.' And the next day Condé lost the battle. In the same way Gide shows how to achieve a failure in *Le Journal des faux-monnayeurs*. Yet Gide is a great writer, even as Condé was a great general. He begins with a turgid Romanticism disguised under the appearances of 'Symbolism.' *Le Voyage d'Urien, Les Nourritures terrestres* would deserve to be completely forgotten were it not that the man who wrote them later came to write *Si le grain ne meurt. L'Immoraliste* marks a progress in style towards simplicity, a progress in spirit towards sincerity. But it only achieves the false simplicity of some Nietzsche, and is also nowadays fallen into disuse.

Les Caves du Vatican would have been a masterpiece (1914) had it been possible not to take it seriously; but unfortunately, under the fantastic tale, there is a moral, or rather an immoral theory: how splendid not to exist, how fine to do things without reason. *L'Acte gratuit* is the maximum effort of mankind. Act without a motive—Kant is dead. Act so that no one else can act as you do. This was to lead to *Les Faux-monnayeurs* and jump clear over Proust. Above all things be a liar—that is truly sublime. If you can—but few can—be a criminal as well, but beware of having a reason for your crime.

In *Les Nourritures terrestres* under the awful Romantic style many of the ideas and sentiments were sound—by which I mean recognizable as human. In *Les Caves* the feelings are upside-down, but the style is becoming clearer and simpler. Perhaps the autobiographical fragment *Si le grain ne meurt* (1924) marks Gide's best period: there his style is openly declared and most effective.

Then a queer thing happened to Gide, and perhaps posterity will decide that there were two writers of the name of André Gide. Can he really have gone to the Congo and to Lake Tchad, and written those two most delightful travel books, *Voyage au Congo* and *Retour du Tchad*? I think those are the books that are most likely to be read for generations; but the later the generation the less it will understand that Gide could write such books. The man who had preached the gospel of *L'Acte gratuit*, homicide without cause or reason, is profoundly shocked because negroes are not well treated. Behind the symbolist poet of André Walter, a long dead romantic humanitarian is now resurrected; a man who cannot bear cruelty to any living things, and who feels that he is a brother to the crocodile and the hippopotamus; a man who reads Milton by moonlight on the Congo river—a delightful man, and who writes like an angel. Why did he have to come back? He should have stayed on the Congo for ever.

The same repressed humanitarianism (rather than politics,

which are not at all in Gide's sphere) took him later on to the Soviet Union. But this produced no literature, and a decent veil should be drawn over the two contradictory statements about the Soviets that came out of the venture. Let us say these were two *actes gratuits*, one for, one against, Communism.

The substance of Gide's writings is, all through, his own self. A *moi* which has not achieved any cohesion, and which, nevertheless, presents itself as on a stage as being everybody's *moi*. Up to a point this claim is justified. Every reader of Gide finds, and fairly often, much of his own self in what is thus presented; mostly parts of himself that the reader has decided long since had better be kept under, and which have become non-important through disuse. The anarchy of youth is made too much of by Gide and his youthful followers. It is really, in the mass of cultured and even of uncultured people, a phase that does not last. Out of the many impulses of their teens as of their early twenties, most men and women choose what they wish to cultivate, what they intend to become; much as they choose a career in the world. Once the career is chosen a human being as a rule does not go back every month to the beginning of yet another career that it might have chosen. In our inner careers we behave in the same way. We decided when fifteen or eighteen or twenty not to be homicidal lunatics; few of us are ever tempted seriously to go back on that decision. Gide is the tempter who offers us again the many careers of crime that we might have adopted. The point is that we did not adopt them and do not intend to go back on that decision. But the picture has an appeal.

The Tchad tales prove that Gide is in a like case. Having chosen a career of intellectual immorality, he sometimes regrets those years of his youth when he could have chosen another career, and he is disturbed about the fate of the negroes as though he were still seventeen, and about the Soviets as though he were still twenty.

In his critical essays he brings out a neat formula, reversing an ancient one (he is practically always in reverse): 'Dieu propose et l'homme dispose'—that is, he says, the basis of

art. God spreads out his creation before us. Man, the
artist, chooses among God's works what he will make into
art. Well, Gide has chosen 'les fleurs du mal' again.

But we should not be busy about Gide (and many will be
for a long time busy about him, as about Benjamin Constant,
or Stendhal) were it not for his achievements as a stylist.
Much of *Si le grain ne meurt*, much of the Tchad stories, much
of *Le Journal*, is a pure delight to read. Many critics hold
that Gide is the greatest writer of French of our time. The
simplicity, the tranquillity, the calm strength of his style put
him among the highest. His style does not suit his ideas at
all. He seems to have obtained it from some separate an-
cestor (he is very proud of the many ancestors he knows—
he is quite a family man really) who had been an artist in the
best times of classical simplicity, some member of the Le
Nain family, who would have nothing to do with the many
other forbears of this much-troubled man: Catholics arguing
against Protestants, unbelievers quarrelling with misbelievers,
moralists chiding at immoralists, and so on.   Apart from them
all, the good workman from a good period, having ousted
from his study that early Romantic and that early pretentious
Symbolist, who made a mess of Walter, Urien, and the Im-
moralist, reigns alone and puts all sorts of moods and ideas—
good or bad, what does he care?—into a perfect form of
French as it exists and breathes in the early twentieth century.
Perhaps that is all that Gide, profoundly, cares about.

It is interesting to note this dichotomy, style—substance,
as it will affect other writers. Some minds express themselves successfully only in form, and a classical form is not
necessarily the sign of an orderly mind. Gide has a most
disorderly mind. So has Anatole France really; so has
Charles Maurras, who sometimes writes admirably. Sometimes one feels that too many French writers in this century
have inherited, and sometimes improved, an ancient form of
art handed over to them and have gone on performing on a
beautiful instrument—but really with nothing to say.

However, there are exceptions: the truly great are exceptions.

PROUST: 1871–1922

Du côté de chez Swann came out in 1913, but was noticed only at the end of the 1914–18 war. Proust's death was a mere accident in 1922, since his long novel went on and *A la recherche du temps perdu* was completed only in 1927. Truly it might be said not to be completed at all since the last volumes are very incomplete. Therein lies the weakness of Proust's art. It is never finished; it is infinitely too long. Another strange contrast with Mallarmé: there is not enough of Mallarmé; there is far too much of Proust. And yet the proportion of good to bad is about the same: say, roughly, one to ten; much the same as with Victor Hugo. Something has gone wrong with art since the eighteenth century: only ten per cent of it is good. Perhaps it is the public who is ninety per cent uneducated and calls upon artists to put ninety per cent mediocrity into their work.

Proust is the encyclopaedia of 'modern' thought, of which the central point, from the literary point of view, is the total disintegration of the self. In this the modern mentality is different from the Romantic as well as from the Classical. In the Classical mood of the seventeenth century *le moi est haïssable*; in good art the writer does not appear. For the Romantics the self was God himself seen in the writer. The love affairs of the poet are the direct concern of the divinity. For Proust and his companions the self as a real entity disappears altogether.

What is the human soul? 'Its essence is reason,' said Descartes. 'Its life is passion, chiefly the passion of love,' said Lamartine.

Proust says: There is no such thing as the human soul; each being carries many souls in itself, all fragile, all temporary. Reason, the intellect? A mere instrument that constructs only errors and delusions. The intellect is always wrong and distorts reality.

Love? A purely imaginative exercise. No doubt painful or blissful, but in no way corresponding to any qualities in the object of love. The object of love is merely a construction of the imagination.

Yet our feelings are real, in so far as we feel them, though not as a link with any outside world. But behind our feelings, more reliable than our feelings, the only true substance of our feelings, are our sensations; chiefly, for Proust, sensual pleasure.

The search for sensual pleasure is the only substance of life.

'Vivent nos sens! Eux ne trompent pas,' writes Montherlant—and that is the modern motto, the basis of Proust's thinking.

Yet sometimes, a few times only in a man's life, there comes through the chaos of his sensations something that has a special quality. The physical world, the origin of our sensations apparently, falls off and an impression of eternity penetrates into our feelings. Once we have felt this eternal sensation we realize that all other sensations do but veil this one and yet lead to it. We go back on our tracks, 'à la recherche du temps perdu,' and discover that this penetration of the divine has been there all the time. The delusion of time disappears; the delusion of the self disappears; space disappears. We are in *Le Temps retrouvé*. We have found the meaning of life.

Thus the goal imagined by Mallarmé is reached by Proust, and in the same way. The cracks in the real, illness, vice, crime, oblivion, the intermittences of the heart, allow the sensation of the eternal to come through. Art is the reconstruction of the process, and the definition of the sensation. That is why art is long; art is too long; art is often dirty as well as drab. Yet it leads to the eternal.

The basis of all this cogitation is Proust's self-disgust. His hero Marcel is an abominable, though apparently charming, creature. He is, no doubt, a slander on Proust, and the mistake of equating the two must not be made. But, standing as he is, Marcel is an abominable creature. He is first of all a constant liar, and his lies are directed to making other people believe that he is a very desirable creature—which he knows quite well he is not. He is a sadist. He enjoys torturing other people—his mother, his grandmother, his various mistresses—with an ultra-refined kind of torture which forces Albertine to run away in simplest self-defence from his monstrous prison. He is truly infernally proud, Satan and Mephistopheles in one, hiding his awful pride under exquisite courtesy—derision so veiled that it seems kindness. A perfect egoist also, next to whom Meredith's egoist is a naïve baby, making himself a burden to his family and friends by a mysterious illness obviously psychological in origin, that is to say, sadistic. Ready to kill anybody by prolonged moral torture to minister to his slightest pleasures; unwilling to let Albertine share the pleasures he derives from her body, so that he truly enjoys himself only when she is asleep. Fidelity is, of course, inconceivable to him.

No wonder Proust recoils in horror from this monster, which is himself, and wishes his self, the self, the human soul, to be dissolved and abolished. He is, as in Mallarmé's *Nuit d'Idumée*:

Ce père essayant un sourire ennemi.

Proust is a satanic archangel sent on earth to purge away his faults by exercising them to exhaustion—and he does it; but his angelic nature comes through at times, luckily. Let us not, however, mistake his nature: it is not human nature. Normal human beings are not made thus. Proust's hero is not a man: he is an illness of human nature, the human soul in decomposition, to be done away with.

The fundamental error of those theologians who want to do away with the self is made obvious in Proust. The abolition of this self does not lead to God; Proust never refers to God. It leads to a pantheism of superhuman but also subhuman forces to which he frequently refers.

Sensualism is his approach to those undesirable divinities.

Desire is first of all of the body, then it is of eternity. There is no place here for the human soul. As soon as desire is satisfied it ceases. After a while it returns, but it is no longer satisfied by what satisfied it first; satiety sets in. A new love is required, to be left again as soon as possessed.

We can truly love, desire, only what we do not possess. Love is the desire for what we lack, and our very being is a lack of being. Love is therefore our normal condition; but love goes to the woman that we cannot have. Love ceases as soon as we have the woman; the craving is only assuaged for a moment, then the monster awakes and looks for another victim. What we possess is of no use to us. And of course the woman we are looking for does not exist; we create entirely out of our own need by our imagination a set of qualities that we transfer on to the beloved, but the beloved has none of them, as we discover as soon as we have her.

Thus Albertine is only bearable while she is absent; held in prison she becomes unbearable and has to run away to become desirable again.

So neither the self of the lover nor the self of the beloved has any continuity, any coherence, any existence.

Now all this is an ache and a nostalgia, and is not true even in Proust's novel. It is as a commentary on a battle by a powerless observer who would be complaining all the time that the soldiers on his side are getting killed all the time, when in fact his army is victorious.

The literary point of view is the true corrective to this excessive cogitation. Is Monsieur de Charlus a pale, incoherent being always on the verge of dissolution, never knowing what he wants, never getting it? Not in the least! Monsieur de Charlus, the greatest creation of Marcel Proust, is an epic personage mixed of Rabelaisian, Cervantesque, and Hugoesque elements: a blusterer in the grand style, a master of irony and a pleasure-seeker of the jolliest, dirtiest, and most persistent kind. The perfect drunkard is nothing to Monsieur de Charlus. He must be read to be believed; but then he is believed. Charlus has made homosexuality into a literary region, as love was before, and caused Gide, who had omitted to die in time, to turn in his immoralism. But

Monsieur de Charlus has none of that self that Proust wishes
to destroy, and none of those glimpses of eternity that
Proust thinks so highly of. In fact, Charlus is totally un-
Proustian.

Then there is no such delightful painter of family life as
Proust. Combray, in Marcel's young days, is a masterpiece.
The grandfather, who is so comically anti-Jewish, the father
whose adored wife is a Jewess, the wife, a trembling image
of faithfulness and delicacy, Marcel's grandmother, true saint
and most admirable soul steeped in love and subtlety. They
are the very opposite of what Proust says human nature is.

Thus the richness of Proust. If we read him with a mind
open, enjoying but resisting his constant lies in depreciation
of human nature, he provides his own remedies. The picture
of the grandmother at death, when the animal and the mineral
forces get hold of her, is unequalled in literature. The dream
in which his father explains that it is no use calling on the
dead grandmother, that her faculties have largely left her,
that she will not know him even, is one of the most penetrating descriptions of bereaved love, equal to Shakespeare
at his best. And Puck, Titania, and all their fairy crew,
with Oberon himself, can only stand in admiration round
Albertine asleep: 'As soon as she slept to some depth, the
plant that lived in her was transfigured; to me, standing dream-
ily on the brink of her sleep, it became a whole countryside.
Her sleep brought to me something as calm, as sensually
penetrating, as the nights of full moon in the bay of Balbec,
quietened as a lake, with branches that move imperceptibly,
when at full length on the sands I would listen endlessly to
the breaking of the descending tide.'

And that famous passage where, as he bends listlessly over
his undone shoe lace, the true realization of his loneliness
now that his grandmother is dead, the true force of his love
of her, overwhelms him and throws him into eternity as a
violent wave might throw him against some ineluctable cliff
—does that prove, as he would have us believe at other times,
that the human heart is weak and feckless? On the contrary,

never has the durability of the soul hidden under daily things been so powerfully vindicated.

Another province he has added to literature is the description of those eternal moments in which we are lifted out of the drab world. Seven or eight times, or ten or twelve times: any reader will discover one or two more. The madeleine dipped in tea, the steeples of Martinville, some trees on a road, a perfume of wild flowers, a vision of light and shade on trees, a spoon clinking on a plate that is like a railway man's hammer on the wheels of the train from which the trees were seen, a stiff napkin in an hotel, an inequality in two stones in Venice and the disjointment in the yard of the Guermantes' town house, and a melody theme out of a great musician's masterpiece. Each of these lead into the eternal.[1]

Such are his masterpieces: Charlus, family life, Albertine asleep, sudden grief, the eternal world, the true characterization and true description.

His pseudo-philosophical cogitations come second only, and are mostly false. The death of Bergotte, for instance, brings thoughts that blend platitude with depth in an unwarrantable way, and that blending mostly mars his thinking.

Lower still must be placed his picture of society. Madame de Guermantes is unconvincing. Surely such a person would die by mummification before she could utter one of her pseudo-witticisms. As for Madame Verdurin, she may be true, but she makes us wish she were not.

With all his faults Proust towers above his period as much as Shakespeare above the Elizabethans. I believe that in the perspective of the future he will appear not perhaps of the size of Balzac, whose genius in the novel is unequalled, but next to Balzac the greatest of the French novelists, one of the same range, as, say, Dostoievsky, and suffering from illnesses that are not Dostoievskian, but that spoil about the same proportion of his work.

[1] *Du côté de chez Swann,* i. 46, 48; 166, 168; *À l'ombre,* i. 63; ii. 19, 21; *Prisonnière,* ii. 243; *Temps retrouvé,* i. 220, 235; ii. 10; ii. 10, 21; ii. 1, 2, 3.

Proust is also a great master of language. Slightly un-French, owing perhaps to his partly Jewish ancestry; slightly muddled up and suffering from indecision in words—often not quite knowing what he means, which makes him so difficult to translate—but with range and power, with a faculty for great rhetoric as well as for pregnant concision. He writes the French of a master who can allow himself some carelessness, some diffusion, some artificiality, because he likes to indulge in those faults, because he knows that at his call the language will come to heel, well trained, and do as it is told.   But let no one attempt to imitate Proust.

THE NOVEL IN THE TWENTIETH CENTURY

WE come now into such a wealth of good novels that it is difficult to classify them. The chronological order is no order. Most of the authors are still alive and, unless each one is taken apart and studied at length for himself, it signifies little that he published this or that in 1910 or in 1930. Some give their best work when young, some in later years. Montherlant, the most Proust-like of the young men, wrote his first book before Proust was at all known. Pierre Hamp, a workman who can write, could be dated 1930, instead of 1910. Duhamel and Romains were full fledged in 1910, but gave their full measure only some twenty years later. Gide covers the whole period. The effect of Proust is nearly retroactive: as soon as writers realize his importance, they react against him. Malraux, Chamson, Giono would feel insulted if they were suspected of imitating Proust—and they would be right. They strive after their own originality.

Nor is there an evolution of the novel. Rather each writer tries to conquer and hold a new field, and invent a new technique. Thibaudet, in a sort of desperate attempt to classify on some real basis, invented, or at least exploited to the full, the notion of 'generation.' But he gets only one generation to play with. He baptizes it the 1914 generation, but he is obliged to put in the emergence of the forty-year-old as masters, and Gide and Proust are pressed into a generation that is not theirs; and yet what can one do? Their great action was round about 1925. There is no order in literature. It might be held that order and literature are antagonistic concepts; each new literary man tries to break away from what he thinks is 'order,' which to him is orthodoxy and death. Thus Racine looked upon Corneille as stereotyped. Thibaudet tries to see three moments after 1914: to 1923, a period of awakening from the war; then 1923 to 1930, inflation; then after 1930, deflation. But he is talking as a

financier. In fact, nearly all new writers were known about
1923–5, and are still alive. Thibaudet's periods are rather
periods in the sale of books than in the creation of works of
art, or in mentality. There is, of course, a sort of connection
between sales and books, but it is a wrong connection, which
vitiates the very idea of art.

There are, nevertheless, similarities between writers, works
of art, points of view, and chiefly ideas. No one can escape
thinking on similar lines to many other people. Some writers
are mouthpieces for groups of people, some others develop
one notion which predecessors just hinted at, and so on.
Connections between writers are so numerous as to be chaotic.
Lack of a set order in development does not come from
isolation in each writer, but of the all too numerous actions
and reactions that take place, not only within the period, but
from previous periods to the later ones. Balzac and Flaubert
and Zola are still active: both because some partly imitate
them, and because some consciously try not to imitate them.

From the now ancient days before 1914 some names still
echo, some works must be read: Pierre Hamp, Eugène Montfort; Jean Richard Bloch, Rosny mark a period of settled
ideas; and just before that war Valéry Larbaud and Alain
Fournier tremble on the brink of a change that was to be
Marcel Proust.

Pierre Hamp invented a new sort of novel—a novel without a tale or a hero, but threaded on an industrial or a trade
cycle, yet fully human. For instance, in *Marée fraîche*, a
typical tale, Hamp begins by the description of the unloading
of the fish at Boulogne. His next scene is the goods station
when the fish is put on the train to Paris, then the fish market
in Paris; then the *restaurants de luxe* where the fish is eaten by
the very rich, and the restaurant kitchen where it is cooked.
But this is not a fishy story: the fish does not matter. At
each point of the cycle Hamp describes the labour and the
character and the habits of the men, women, and children
whose lives are spent on, and living earned by, handling the
commodity.

Then Hamp does it again and again: *Le Lin*, *Le Rail* give admirable—and true—descriptions of the lives of factory workers and their magnates; of railway men and great administrators. The formula is fruitful, and made to live by the fact that Pierre Hamp was a workman, a somewhat loose yet successful stone that rolled through many trades and lived to tell.

He writes a bad kind of thoroughly racy and true French, much as the people speak, and fascinates the reader by the revelation of how the poor—and the rich—live. Whether he is ever forgotten or not, he is sure of being resuscitated in future centuries by people who will want to know how the French masses really did live about 1900.

Eugène Montfort has written many pleasant books, chiefly about towns. Marseilles, Naples, some parts of Paris, live as entities in his work; but his one appendix to literature—rather than contribution to it—is *La Turque*, the life-story of a prostitute, which beats Zola or any previous adventurer in that unknown world. Montfort seems to know.

In this world of hard labour (in both senses) Jean Richard Bloch's novel, *Et compagnie*, holds high rank. It tells how some Jews from Alsace, after the war of 1870, came to Normandy to establish a textile factory, and how they won both reputation and money. But in Bloch work does not really come first: the necessity of continuing the race is the first motive, the part played by the women in maintaining the mentality of the family through generations, the tyranny of the old men in business and life, and the downfall and dispersal of the tribe when the great old men disappear. The process then to start anew elsewhere.

Jean Richard Bloch later on wandered into fairy-tales in Asia Minor (*Nuit kurde*) and into the drama (*Le Dernier Empereur*), or the long-range novel (*Sybilla*), but to most readers *Et Cie* remains his most solid work.

Rosny carried on the fairy-tale attempt into prehistoric times. *La Guerre du feu* is a pleasant winter's tale. It is true that the more we learn about the savages of to-day, the less we are inclined to believe Rosny, whose prehistoric savages are rather very early rationalists and agnostics; but such were the limitations of 1900. That must not stop any reader who is prepared to enjoy a good evening in the supposed simplicity of the beginnings of mankind. And Rosny has written many such very good tales.

But simplicity was now on its death-bed. The war of 1914 and Marcel Proust were on the way: not as causes, either of them, but as symptoms. Valéry Larbaud, with *Barnabooth*, strikes a note that will grow into whole symphonies with Paul Morand, Giraudoux, and Maurois, and even Michaux. Here a group affiliation is noticeable. Fantasy, extensive travelling, and eccentricity, with a sadistic undercurrent, make up a witty but rather undesirable *genre*. Gide and Proust are not far.

Fantasy, too, is the chief note of Alain Fournier's *Le Grand Meaulnes*, which has a grand start and then rather flounders to an unfortunate ending. A wonderful tale of a child wandering unwarned into a world of theatricals in a big country house, and mixing up reality and make-believe— really only matter for a short story, yet instinct with a sense of heart-break. All who are wistfully inclined should be loyal to *Le Grand Meaulnes*, at least for fifty pages, which may be transmitted down literary anthologies.

The war of 1914–18 did produce three or four good books. Barbusse was a revelation: *Le Feu* came out during the war in a daily newspaper as a serial—as a compendium of the impressions and reactions of a good humanitarian heart at the front. It remains probably the greatest of war books. It is not really a book: it is the outpouring into language of the feelings of an outraged human heart. Dorgelès's *Les Croix de bois* is a more composed work of art and more of a document. Duhamel's *La Vie des martyrs* deals with the sufferings of the wounded from a very human doctor's point of view, and, later, Jules Romains's *Verdun* was to be a sort of final summing-up—from the bench this time, not from a witness.

After the war, perhaps, we received our first warning blow that much was changed from Paul Morand. *Ouvert la nuit* was a revelation that somehow scandalized us. Was this a new mentality? These people who made love as they made money, and left a mistress much as a business man goes into liquidation? Illness and revolution; Irish patriotism as a destructive force; Communism in Barcelona—the human heart had disappeared; the human senses and vices were holding high revelry. We understood only a little later, when we had had time to consider Proust and the 'modern' moods.

Meanwhile, Maurois enchanted us for a while. Colonel Bramble made us forget the seriousness of things, and perhaps lulled us into a respect for the unconscious powers that was a great delusion. In truth Colonel Bramble does not represent the English at all. It is a very good joke, comparable to the very good jokes made in Aberdeen. We shall continue to enjoy it, but this war has made it rather painful at times. *Climats* and *Le Cercle de famille* give Maurois a greater scope as true novels, but somehow are not quite successful. The fantastic vein in Maurois is developed and comes off best in his semi-scientific tales, like *La Machine à lire la pensée*, which has a true Voltairean atmosphere. Perhaps that is Maurois's true vocation.

Giraudoux is an even more fantastic dreamer. His *Siegfried* bears a very dubious meaning: Could a Frenchman become a Hitler in Germany? It was written before Hitler came, and it was a very false prophecy. *Suzanne et le Pacifique* turned Robinson Crusoe upside down and inside out; but no one could say 'We are not amused.' We were. Are we still? The *Bella* series now have an after-taste. Poincaré? His adversaries? Perhaps we had that tale told us in the wrong way. Here again the events of 1940 knock some of the inter-war writing out of both reality and literature.

If you are going to write historical novels you must be careful to establish some connection with reality, especially if your history is present in every one's sensibility. History, to be made into a joke, demands a kind of literary genius that has not yet arisen. So far, even good writers had better leave history to the journalists, while waiting for true historians —of whose coming there are no symptoms.

More serious workmen were engaged in writing more serious works. Out of many good books by Jean Schlumberger, *Saint-Saturnin* stands out as one of the best novels of our time. The theme is simple, and in France, as elsewhere, based on a frequent and unpleasant piece of reality: the weakening of the mind and heart of an old man, who yet remains the master of the property and therefore of the destinies of his family. How the young generation reacts and wins makes a good story, but the talent of the writer reaches complete success in the description of the life of the house and the *domaine* in Normandy. As a piece of true picturing of the innermost life of France *Saint-Saturnin*, with its simple and most effective French, stands as a permanent acquisition to literature.

Jacques Chardonne became known by his *Épithalame*. No one has truly succeeded in giving a picture of married life. Perhaps the subject, like many most important subjects, does not lend itself to literature—for it is a great mistake to think that literature can deal with all subjects. Only a very small number of themes in every age are literary, and that small number vary in every age. For instance, descriptions of eating and drinking used to be literature, and have ceased to be. Yet *Épithalame* does give some results—which is an achievement. Later, in the series of *Les Destinées sentimentales* (*Porcelaine de Limoges*), Chardonne succeeded in a picture of provincial life, in which business, local *mœurs*, and love in and out of marriage are very artistically combined.

Jouhandeau must be mentioned in this matter of marriage. His M. Godeau, who is married to a sort of saint, is a horrible experience in reading. But for subtlety, sadism, and amazing French, Jouhandeau can out-Proust Proust himself. But how many readers can bear to go into the unknown further than Proust has taken them? Great intelligence overreaches itself, and falls on the other side of its target as an arrow that goes too far and does not hit what it was meant to hit. As an exercise in subtlety, depth, and all the terrible qualities, Jouhandeau's work is a challenge to all readers that think themselves cultured. Not that in any way he imitates Proust. He lives in a different country, in the same continent, but further still from us.

As Henry Michaux does, whose name is enough. Cruelty should not be encouraged nowadays: there is already too much of it.

Lacretelle, with his *Hauts Ponts* series—a study in the heredity of imagination—can be classed with Chardonne and Schlumberger as a source of genuine literary pleasure, but Martin du Gard with *Les Thibault* ranks rather with Michaux and Jouhandeau as an analyst of most unpleasant things. Perhaps human nature is not generally so horrible as all that.

That it is horrible, however, the Catholic novelists agree. Two important writers, Mauriac and Bernanos, stand firmly on the Roman Catholic position, and are severe critics of fallen humanity.

Mauriac is the more purely literary writer, as Bernanos is liable to go off into pamphlets of a rather unpleasant kind against his own people. Mauriac's *Désert de l'amour*, *Thérèse Desqueyroux*, *Le Nœud de vipères* give an unexampled true picture of the Catholic bourgeoisie, of the propertied classes in the south-west of France. All his characters are unpleasant, and their Catholicism merely serves to give them a profound sense of sin, which they can be suspected of enjoying—and Mauriac is not guiltless in this. He could be accused of being partial to sin—and a rather monotonous kind of sin. But from a purely literary point of view he is a veritable Loti of the lands of the south-west. The pines of the Landes are to him what the sea is to Loti, and it is pleasant to recall that by writing *Ramuntcho* Loti made himself beforehand Mauriac's next-door neighbour. But Ramuntcho is a Basque and a man of the mountains; Mauriac's country bourgeois are in the plains and the resinous odorous trees. A road near Bordeaux, a spring among the pines, smells on a countryside, an old servant in an old house—Mauriac makes them unforgettable, and his French is one of the most sensitive languages even penned.

As for Bernanos, he is a giant of the Catholics. Be on your guard when you meet him. When *Sous le soleil de Satan* appeared many said that a maniac had arisen in literature. But *L'Imposture*, the portrait of the inner soul of an unbelieving priest, is a masterpiece in every way—not unlike Duhamel's *Salavin* in its capacity for soul revelation, though totally unlike: the priest of *L'Imposture* should have been Salavin's confessor, that is all. In *La Joie* Bernanos tried to reveal a saint: a truly pure and suffering young girl who is in God. The subject is profoundly interesting. None but Bernanos could have attempted it, but even he does not quite cover it. The people who surround the young virgin are more alive than she is. The curious situation of Flaubert's *Salammbô* is thus repeated in modern days. The same sacrifice ends the book. The tremendous pamphlets, *La Grande Peur des bien pensants*, *Les Cimetières sous la lune*, must be read soon to be appreciated. It is to be feared that another generation will be unable to understand them at all; some of the style may still hit—but we are dangerously near journalism which cannot be made into literature.

Montherlant is the Rimbaud of the novel of the 1920s; he is the bad boy who is a portent; he is to Proust what Rimbaud had been to Mallarmé. All that was to come out fully in the greater writer is already chaotic in him. It is visible in his war book *Le Songe*, written when he was nineteen, in 1919 or so. It is tumultuously expressed in his one good book, *Les Bestiaires*, a story of bulls and bull-people in Spain, and his *essais-récits*, *La Petite Infante de Castille*, *Aux sources du désir*. He is as yet unconscious of Proust when Proust is already upon us, whereas all the novelists so far mentioned are pre-Proust or para-Proust; and the younger men coming, Malraux, Chamson, Giono, Céline, are post-Proust and rather anti-Proust. Montherlant is the proof that Proust is typical of a period and a mentality; he is a specimen of the Proust young. He is

Robert de Saint-Loup come to life. He is the proof that
Paul Morand, Giraudoux, Maurois, Mauriac, and Bernanos
(for he is a good Catholic) are really all varieties within one
species. A few quotations are necessary and sufficient to put
Montherlant in his place, for he never quite achieved a success
in a work of art as such except in *Les Bestiaires*. But here he
is speaking more clearly than Proust, knowing better than
Proust himself what Proust is after—for he is more courageous,
more outspoken than Proust. As the best definitions of
Romanticism are in Musset, who is a young man to the great
Romantics, so the best definitions of the 'modern' mentality
are in Montherlant, a youth to Gide and Proust and Valéry,
a youth who tells the truth brazenly and recklessly. Sensations are the only truth.

'Et aujourd'hui comme hier, je répète ma profession de
foi, faite aussi dans *Le Songe*: Vivent nos sens! Eux ne
trompent pas.'

'On dit que se livrer au plaisir c'est s'étourdir. C'est tout
le contraire. Le plaisir étant la seule vérité, c'est se livrer
à autre chose qu'à lui, c'est se livrer à autre chose que la
vérité, qui est s'étourdir.'

The intellect is a third-rate and insignificant instrument.

'Je n'ai jamais passé de l'acte de jouir à l'acte de comprendre sans avoir la sensation nette que je passais de la
sagesse à la folie—par les sens j'atteins une solution. Par
l'esprit je n'en atteindrai jamais une: on ne peut comprendre
sans se tromper. Voilà pourquoi je dis et je redis que seuls
les sens ne dupent pas.'

But sensation dies quickly—then *l'ennui*, the emptiness of
the soul, has us. The fifteen volumes of Proust in four
sentences:

'La seule ombre sur ce jardin était celle de mon monstre
intérieur, au gros ventre, au membre flasque, aux yeux clos,
à la lèvre bavante de sauces, et qui a nom Satiété. Salaud,
lui disais-je, tu vas m'avoir tout de même. Satiété de corps,
qui finissait par bonnement refuser comme un cheval qui
refuse de boire advantage. Satiété de l'âme.'

Therefore we can love only what we do not possess; what we possess we no longer love. See Albertine and Marcel.

'Cette ville tuée par l'ennui, c'est moi-même. Ah, soupirais-je, quand serons-nous débarrassés des êtres adorables !'

'Qu'on me croie, si je le possédais (Dieu) j'en aurais vite assez de lui !'

'Ce qui m'enivrait, c'était le sombre vin de l'absurde, la tentation malsaine de me faire mal et de me mutiler sans but.'
Here goes Gide and *Le Crime gratuit* !

As for *le moi*, away with it:

'J'assiste avec terreur à moi-même — je comprends maintenant pourquoi on l'a appelé le grand pourrisseur. Cette soif de l'anéantissement — le néant est vraiment la grande espérance.'

Truth? No, the kingdom of the fairies:

'Je ne crois et n'espère qu'en la féerie — il n'y a que la féerie qui vaille d'être prise au sérieux.' Enter Giraudoux.
Enter Supervielle, and *L'Enfant de la haute mer*.

Love? What is it? 'Dans la vie aussi, des êtres se substituent, se chassent l'un l'autre de nos bras, sans que nous paraissions nous en apercevoir.'

Hence cruelty, sadism: to escape *l'ennemi*, to escape *le moi*, to escape love. 'Les amants mêlent à leurs caresses les morsures et les coups ! Les primitifs chassent et tuent le fauve qu'ils adorent.—Je lui trouvais mille grâces parce que je savais que dans deux heures il ne serait plus.—J'avais rendu à la vie son pathétique.'

Sensation dies; pain dies last; the pleasure to inflict pain is the most durable of pleasures. Hence wars. Hence this war twenty years after Montherlant thought this out. This war was a necessity of the 'modern' mentality: one has to feel something or else one does not live. Cruelty can be the ultimate thing to feel.

Therefore after Montherlant comes Malraux. Cruelty as the constructive power for the building of a new world. *Les Conquérants* came as a surprise in the novel when we thought we could no longer be surprised. China is the traditional land for the legend of cruelty.   How do the heroes live, kill, and die?   Now Proust, as a setting sun, has disappeared below the horizon—Malraux has nothing to do with Proust or Montherlant—he comes later.   We shall now hear how the great Communist heroes took China.   This is not politics— it is only a human tale.   What happened to men when a great man came south?   Never mind what he wanted; what happened?   Malraux tells.   And he tells equally well what happened when the Communists were exterminated in Shanghai, in *La Condition humaine*; or what happened in Spain in *L'Espoir*. His capacity for taking politics for granted and telling the human tale of men and women who are utterly devoted to a cause is a truly rare power, beyond the generation of Barrès and France.   In *La Voie royale* he devotes this power to the description of a thief that wants to take away the old statues of the Khmer and sell them.   The emotions of a thief, or of a bandit, are emotions; the objects round which they move are of little import in themselves.

André Chamson is a sort of home Malraux.   His *Hommes de la route* give a solid picture of what happens in the Cévennes when great work is on hand.   *La Galère* tells of the Paris police in times of revolution nowadays; Malraux's Shanghai is no better than Chamson's Paris.   Lack of charity also begins at home.   But how much more tragic Malraux and Chamson than were, a generation before, France and Barrès with their Dreyfus or Panama affairs: those were early symptoms of a curable disease.   Malraux and Chamson tell of the last spasms of a dying world.   Yet both have greater hopes than their predecessors—they look to an ardent future where Barrès and France looked to decomposition.   Malraux calls the Spanish war *L'Espoir*.   Later even than Malraux appear Giono and Céline: the power of the earth and the decomposition of mankind; after which the 1940 war was necessary.

Giono has lit up the French Alps. *Un de Beaumugues*, *Regain*, *Batailles dans la montagne*, many more great books, show how man is only a bit of the earth, and the earth is a spiritual power that moves slowly or instantaneously, but far transcends human life and love. *Le Grand Troupeau* is made of sheep, but also of men at war. The ram dies of having to walk too quickly down to the plains again, for a terrible, mysterious, and precise reason. Shall man die also for some similar reason? The shepherds on the higher pastures of the Alps, in *Le Serpent d'étoiles* and *Le Chant du monde*, cut the highest trees into Aeoliah harps, and the music of the spheres comes through to the mountain tops. But it is a secret that few know about, and it must not be spread. Mankind may be going to die. It does not matter: there are better things than mankind in the beyond and the hereafter. An amazing poet, who could have belonged to the Himalayas or to high Peru, but who happens to be in the French Alps and to write French with the best—and there have been many masters in that best.

As for Céline, it is fitting to draw the veil somewhere, and also to draw the line. He has utterly divested himself of shame, and he is also a great poet. He has written two tremendous books and then sunk out of literature and become a Rabelaisian pamphleteer—against the Jews. His *Voyage au bout de la nuit* contains some of the most amazing (the word must be repeated, even after Giono)—some of the most amazing writing since Rabelais. The hero, after escaping from the war where he was a heroic figure, goes to Africa and there becomes lost to the world in the Rio del Oro. He is actually transhipped to America on a kind of prehistoric galley—and becomes an inspector-general in charge of the insects that are brought to the new continent on the skins of immigrants. The reader ceases to believe, ceases to understand, but is carried on into a description of the amazing (again) beauty of American women and of a Ford factory. The writer himself no longer knows what is happening. A marvellous madman has taken charge of the novel. Fantastic, unreal, mad? All right, says Céline, wait and see. And he writes *Mort à crédit*. There he tells Paris and London (and Chatham) what he thinks of them. A prehistoric galley was a paradise, and the insects on the immigrants were angels as compared with what you see and hear in Paris alleys or London boarding-houses. And then there is a dog: a good dog—but he had seen so much of man's behaviour that he had lost his nerve. He went away from mankind, altogether, as a judgment, as only a dog could.

It must be read to be believed, and it was time 1940 came to put an end to that period. But what a period! It was our nerve that failed, like the dog's. From Mallarmé to Céline—no greater ambit could be imagined, and every point of the compass had been gone through: poetry could be no subtler, prose could be no grosser. What ever can be done now? Yet the human mind has to go on.

NOTE: Mention must be made of Ramuz, a Swiss writer, and of Hémon, a Breton turned Canadian—both of very high merit in form and substance; Hémon's *Maria Chapdelaine* is a sort of classic; Ramuz might be called the Hémon of Switzerland. Ignace Legrand, the only French novelist who came to England and stayed there during this war, has an originality of his own, looking at the French as though from outside France (*La Patrie intérieure, Renaissance*).

PAUL VALÉRY: 1871–1945

Paul Valéry was one of those who listened to Mallarmé regularly from 1892. He made a few attempts in the Mallarméan technique—not very successful—and in 1895 wrote a portrait of the master, *La Soirée avec Monsieur Teste*, in which the great man is well presented as reduced to silence by the power and subtlety of his own thinking—a slightly ironical presentation, however, the irony of which is, while remaining· friendly, emphasized later in the complete volume on Monsieur Teste. Madame Teste is here introduced, with her thoughts about her husband, in one of the most delightful pieces in the French language.

But then obviously Paul Valéry himself had some thinking to do, and withdrew from the world of literature. Inappropriately enough he re-entered it in the middle of the first world war with a masterpiece, *La Jeune Parque* (1917), which is really a resetting of *L'Après-midi d'un faune*, Mallarmé's most sustained effort. From the start he beat Mallarmé, both in power of expression and in density of good poetry.

Charmes (1922, 1926), which became *Poésies* by the addition of *La Jeune Parque* and (a rather unnecessary one) of Valéry's first poems (*L'Album de vers anciens*, dating back to 1892–3), is nevertheless a slight volume, less than Baudelaire's, hardly longer than Mallarmé's. But practically everything in it ·is good, which, as we have stated already, is far from being the case with the earlier masters.

Mallarmé had failed to make good, but Valéry has made good for him. All of Mallarmé's ideas are carried out triumphantly in Valéry. Whereas hardly one poem of Mallarmé's, however short, is good all through, Valéry's poems, even quite long ones like *La Jeune Parque* or *Le Cimetière marin*, are excellent poetry throughout. In fact, but for Valéry, we could hold that Mallarmé had talked only brilliant

nonsense.   Valéry proved that it could be done—although
it took him some thirty years to do it.

Valéry is not only the successful expression of Mallarmé,
though that would be enough to make him great; he is,
besides, the poetical, orderly, and concise expression of those
'modern' ideas, which Proust was attempting at the same
time to put into prose.   But Proust failed to be either orderly
or concise, and, if he achieved poetical expression at times, it
was in the halting medium of a prose that was sometimes
invertebrate and sometimes endowed with too many vertebrae.
Valéry is a true poet, that is, one who writes in magnificent
verse.   Also he is a healthy man—at least compared with
Proust.   He is a pessimist, of course, as the 'modern' man
who does not believe in God is bound to be.   But his
pessimism is beautiful and strong:

> Maigre immortalité noire et dorée,
> Consolatrice affreusement laurée
> Qui de la mort fais un sein maternel,
> Le beau mensonge et la pieuse ruse —
> Qui ne connaît et qui ne les refuse,
> Ce crâne vide et ce rire éternel?

La Jeune Parque tells of the dissolution of the self, seeking that
serpent, sensation, through the inner forests of the soul:

> J'ai de mes bras épais environné mes tempes,
> Et longtemps de mon âme attendu les éclairs.
> Toute? — en mes doux liens, à mon sang suspendue
> Je me voyais me voir sinueuse, et dorais
> De regards en regards mes profondes forêts.
> — J'y suivais un serpent qui venait de me mordre.
> — Adieu, pensai-je, moi, mortelle sœur, mensonge.

Here is at last perfect poetry, with a form worthy of great
substance, such as had not been heard since Victor Hugo.
In the true line of Hugo, too, and Hugo was in the main
current, having received as co-tributaries both Boileau and
Ronsard.   In *Le Cimetière marin*, that splendid piece, such
lines as these about the dead:

> Ils ont fondu dans une absence épaisse,
> L'argile rouge a bu la blanche espèce,
> Le don de vivre a passé dans les fleurs,

are a restatement, nearly as successful in a minor key as
the grand original, of Hugo's *Pleurs dans la nuit* when the poet
bids the earth, *l'argile rouge*, take the dead one and transform
him:

> Terre! fais-en des fleurs! des lys que l'aube arrose
> — Fais ruisseler ce sang dans tes sources d'eaux vives
> Et fais le boire aux bœufs mugissants, tes convives
> — Fais-en des buissons verts, fais-en de grandes herbes
> — Fais avec tous ces morts une joyeuse vie.

This gigantic exuberance is altogether beyond Valéry, but in
his slimmer and more aristocratic elegance he can say nearly
as much:

> Le don de vivre a passé dans les fleurs.

And he can reach the height of Hugo, though not to stay on
it for long.

> Mais dans leur nuit toute lourde de marbres
> Un peuple vague, aux racines des arbres
> A déjà pris ton parti lentement.

He sings the negative mood, Proust-like, where Hugo sings
the positive mood, but, like Hugo again, he can sweep the
strings in the rarefied air of philosophical poetry. Listen to
his *No*, against which we shall set Hugo's richer *Yes*; the
No is not unworthy of the *Yes*:

> Soleil, soleil! . . . Faute éclatante
> — Tu gardes les cœurs de connaître
> Que l'Univers n'est qu'un défaut
> Dans la pureté du Non-Être.

> L'immense espoir de fruits amers
> Affole les fils de la fange
> — Cette soif qui te fit géant
> Jusqu'à l'Être exacte l'étrange
> Toute-Puissance du Néant!

Thus the serpent in *Charmes*. But compare Hugo on the
other register, and you can see that Valéry is a worthy con-
tradictor of the high priest.

Hugo writes in *La Lumière*, in *Dieu*, answering Valéry before Valéry was born.

> Ceux qui sont dans la nuit ont raison quand ils disent,
> Rien n'existe! Car c'est dans un rêve qu'ils sont.
>
> Rien n'existe que lui, le flamboiement profond
> Et les âmes, les grains de lumière, les mythes,
> Les moi mysterieux —

To be contradicted thus is a true sign of greatness, on both sides. But Valéry contradicts older, perhaps greater, sages than Hugo. In his prose masterpiece, *Eupalinos* (1923), again one of the grandest pieces in the French language, he tramples down the highest flowers of Proust, and affronts Plato himself in a delirium of iconoclasm. Plato aspires to a reminiscence and a vision of the ideas, Proust has glimpses of the eternal forces which surely are connected with the Platonic ideas. Paul Valéry boldly asks: How am I to know that these supreme sensations are not deceiving me?

'Les puissances accourent. Tu sais bien que les puissances de l'âme procèdent étrangement de la nuit. Elles avancent, par illusion, jusqu'au réel. Ces faveurs surabondantes et mystérieuses, loin de les accueillir telles quelles, uniquement déduites du grand désir, naïvement formées de l'extrême attente de mon âme, il faut que je les arrête, ô Phèdre, et qu'elles attendent mon signal. Et les ayant obtenues par une sorte d'interruption de ma vie (adorable suspens de l'ordinaire durée), je veux encore que je divise l'indivisible, et que je tempère et que j'interrompe la naissance même des idées — c'est qu'il m'importe sur toute chose, d'obtenir de ce qui va être, qu'il satisfasse, avec toute la vigueur de sa nouveauté, aux exigences raisonnables de ce qui a été.' 'Quand tu penses, ne sens-tu pas que tu déranges secrètement quelque chose?'

You have to go back to Bossuet to find such writing in prose.

Yet one word of caution is necessary. Valéry has a tendency to depreciate himself. His masterpieces are, in verse, all contained in a small volume, *Poésies*; two volumes,

Monsieur Teste and *Eupalinos*, are masterpieces in prose. But he has explained in too many articles, lectures, and essays that *Le Cimetière marin* really is only the filling-in with words of no importance of a metric pattern that came to him suddenly, and not a very original pattern, either. The irony of *La Soirée avec Monsieur Teste* turns inwards a little too tellingly. The wit of innumerable aphorisms, published in all too numerous small volumes, is apt to take the great thoughts downhill and dash them into fragments at the bottom of the descent. There is a sort of destructive power at work, both in the poet and in the thinker, just as there is in Baudelaire, in Rimbaud, in Mallarmé, and in Proust. In a better period, in one that had a more constructive spirit, Valéry could have been another Bossuet or another Hugo. Perhaps it is because of us that *Le Cimetière marin* is in lines of ten syllables, *un peu maigre*, instead of lines of twelve syllables, as all other great poetry is, in French.

A certain lack of substance; too much hesitation in the acceptance of life and of death; a certain lack of generosity. The wings are there—is the power there? Why are the flights so short? A certain lack of strength. He had adopted the negative mode, therefore his song is thinner as well as less fantastic than Hugo's. Little courage comes from him except of the Vigny kind, the calm courage of despair, which is mostly a pose, though a noble one, and sometimes a fake.

Yet, when all is said, the greatest recent poet, the greatest poet since Hugo. The best prose writer, since when? The best expression of our times, and we have a right to be proud of him perhaps. He is true to our times, when the negative is dominant. At least he gives it form and beauty.

SUPERVIELLE

SUPERVIELLE is one of the 'hopeful' symptoms of the 'modern' school. Whereas little but pessimism can be deduced from Proust, Gide, and even Valéry, Supervielle represents all the 'modern' tendencies in them and yet is a normal human being, and one who looks upward and forward with some degree of strength and confidence. He is perhaps even more purely a poet than Paul Valéry. Valéry has always some philosophical idea lurking round the corner of a stanza; Supervielle deals only in poetic impressions and never attempts to convince himself or his reader of any truth. Here is *Sans Dieu* in his *Forçat innocent*, perhaps his best collection of poems:

> J'avance entre les astres avec deux chiens aveugles
> Qui parfois se rapprochent pour chercher mon chemin.
> On ne voit rien ici qui ressemble à la Terre.
> — Le ciel tout près de moi me tourmente et me ment.
> Il m'a pris mes deux chiens gelés restés derrière
> Et j'entends leur exsangue immobile aboiement.
> — O ciel, ciel abaissé, je te touche des mains,
> Et m'enfonce voûté dans la céleste mine —

That is the answer—an answer of strength and hope—to Valéry's *Sans Dieu* idea:

> Le beau mensonge et la pieuse ruse —

'Let us go and see,' says Supervielle.

And here is his answer to Proust's despairing contentions that we can never reach the woman we love. It is not irrelevant to note that Proust was not a normal human being, and knew not of marriage or of parenthood—the only child he knew was himself. But Supervielle is lover, husband, and father, and the human processes appear as a whole in proper perspective to him:

> Vivante ou morte, ô toi qui me connais si bien,
> Laisse-moi t'approcher à la façon des hommes.
> — Ah! que j'arrête un jour ta chair à la dérive,
> Toi qui vas éludant ton désir et le mien
> Au large de mes mains, qu'escortent des abîmes.—

Man and woman do meet, and children come, and that is the framework of life and of love; taking a small fragment, like the desire before mating, and nothing else, is of no use to the poet. Poetry as a criticism of life needs to transcend and enclose the whole of life, which neither Proust nor Valéry do. Supervielle does. He is *le moderne sain*, whereas Proust is *le moderne malade*, and Valéry is the modern under treatment, being his own doctor, with many useless cures.

Similarly as regards cruelty and Gide. Cruelty has had a renaissance in literature. What more natural in the world of 1914–18 and of 1940? The later Romantics had been partly sadists and told *contes cruels* in a humanitarian world. But in the twentieth century you do not have to be a sadist. You do not have to create suffering—there is more than you need—but you must face cruelty, and give it a place in the cosmos. Thus Proust is wickedly cruel in the spiritual world; Gide invents *Le Crime gratuit*; Valéry's *Jeune Parque* says:

> Je suivais un serpent qui venait de me mordre.

But all of them are afraid of cruelty because it has slipped its leash; it ranges lawlessly over the world.

Not so Supervielle, who goes back to the centre and beginning: cruelty in children, which is not cruelty. He is the only Frenchman who can run along the terrible paths across which Blake's tiger ranges. Thus both Proust and Gide with their cruelty appear, under Supervielle's gaze, as what they really are: children who have omitted, rather deliberately, to grow up. Here is *Le Voyage difficile*, which must be given complete:

> Sur la route une charrette,
> Dans la charrette un enfant
> Qui ne veut baisser la tête
> Sous des cahots surprenants.
>
> La violence de la route
> Chasse l'attelage au loin,
> D'où la terre n'est que boule
> Dans le grand ciel incertain.

Ne parlez pas: c'est ici
Qu'on égorge le soleil.
Douze bouchers sont en ligne,
Douze coutelas pareils.

Ici l'on saigne la lune
Pour lui donner sa pâleur.
L'on travaille sur l'enclume
Du tonnerre et de l'horreur.

'Enfant, cache ton visage,
Car tu cours de grands dangers.
— Ne vois-tu pas, étranger,
Que j'ai un bon attelage?'

Garçons des autres planètes,
N'oubliez pas cet enfant
Dont nous sommes sans nouvelles
Depuis déjà très longtemps.

And all the cruelty of the world is in *L'Enfant de la haute mer*,
the most marvellous story in the language.   How wrong that
Flemish sailor was to concentrate on the image of his dead
little daughter at midnight in mid-ocean, for the child had to
come back and live immortally in the wastes of the Atlantic,
alone and for ever going through the gestures and avocations
of her small life, in spite of her yearning heart and of the
kindness of the waves.   Cruelty in the world of men is
integrated into the cosmic necessities:

Ici on saigne la lune
Pour lui donner sa pâleur.

The moon has to be pale, therefore there must be bleeding;
the child will attend to it.

As for *le moi*, the famous romantic *moi*, the infamous
Proustian or Gidean *moi*, Supervielle is not to be fooled by
the antics of *le moi*, all mountebank tricks.   There is a deep
self that remains obdurate and untouched (*Ruptures*):

Moi de Montevideo,
Ne me tourne pas le dos.
— Avons-nous vraiment fini
De nous croire bons amis?

Intermittences du cœur, says Proust.   Supervielle answers: *Intermittences de la terre* (in *Le Forçat innocent*).   Art remains when life is gone: this is better than *Le Temps retrouvé*:

> Dans la forêt sans heures
> On abat un grand arbre.
> Un vide vertical
> Tremble en forme de fût,
> Près du tronc étendu.
>
> Cherchez, cherchez, oiseaux,
> La place de vos nids,
> Dans ce haut souvenir
> Tant qu'il murmure encore.

RHYME AND REASON

FRENCH poetry, after the two extraordinary efforts of the classical drama and of the romantic lyric, has become tired of its old instrument, the twelve-syllable rhymed couplet with alternate masculine and feminine endings. After Racine, after Hugo and Leconte de Lisle, what could one write in that form that would not be mere repetition? Anna de Noailles, one of the most popular of all poets, reads merely like a feminine and still more inexhaustible Lamartine. There is still much appetite among the public for this kind of form in poetry, but many poets feel stultified by it. Verlaine registered protest, as is well known, in his *Art poétique*:

Oh, qui dira les torts de la rime —

And right down to Aragon, who adds to his *Crève-cœur* in 1943 a note of rhyme at the present day, a number of poets have tried either to do away with rhyme or so to change its role as to renew poetic form.

Supervielle says that he neither fears rhyme nor looks for it. Let it come naturally, or not come naturally. In the *Voyage difficile* we note, as endings: *charrette, tête, enfant, surprenants; route, boule, loin, incertain* (which is much less of a rhyme); *ici, ligne* (which is nothing but *i*) and *soleil, pareil* (orthodox); *lune, enclume* (a bad rhyme), *pâleur, horreur* (orthodox); *visage, attelage; dangers, étranger* (orthodox); *planètes, nouvelles* (no rhymes, but an *è*); *enfant, longtemps* (a rhyme, but weak). In the *forêt* poem we find: *heure, arbre, vertical* (no rhyme), *fût, étendu* (very weak); *oiseau, nids* (no rhyme); *souvenir, encore* (just an *r*). So truly the freedom of the poet is full, and *les torts de la rime* are set aside. Supervielle has solved his problem. Less rhyme and much reason go together.

But Éluard writes:

Sans âge

Nous approchons
Dans les forêts.
Prenez la rue du matin,
Montez les marches de la brume.
Nous approchons.
La terre en a le cœur crispé.

Encore un jour à mettre au monde.

A delicate poem. But why a poem? Why not prose? You can cut up Chateaubriand (and it has often been done) in the same way, or even, as that awful Stendhal pointed out, the *Code civil*. What then will be the difference between prose and poetry?

The answer has been growing since Baudelaire: poetry is less *raisonnable* than prose. When Rimbaud gave up rhyme he had to give up reason: otherwise *Une Saison en enfer* would be prose. Éluard is gingerly trying to give up reason—a difficult task—in

Prenez la rue du matin.

But he does not quite succeed: it is explainable.

But this is a long story, and goes back to Verlaine's contemporaries—not important enough to make each a separate mark, but occupying a poetic region of great fascination between or round Verlaine and Rimbaud. Tristan Corbière (*Les Amours jaunes*), Lautréamont (*Chants de Maldoror*) (Thibaudet calls him 'un fou'), Jules Laforgue, René Ghil. All disorderly, but at times powerful attempts to renew poetic form, but also to make the substance of poetry so unproselike that it did not matter whether you wrote in verse or not. Chaos was the result, and none of these poets really count: self-sacrifices in poetic exploration. Just before the 1914 war things came to a second crisis, and the joint attempt to give up both rhyme and reason—one loss balancing the other—produced Apollinaire (*Calligrammes*), another inspiring failure, followed by many surrealists and others, a first Aragon (very different from the patriotic Aragon of 1942),

Breton, Soupault, Cocteau, Éluard. This movement reached
a sort of religious fanaticism, and men like Supervielle,
Fargue, were regarded as traitors to it. Unfortunately the
traitors succeeded better than the others. Very little poetry
was produced in this way, and Éluard, with the few lines
quoted above, will have to serve as a specimen.

There is a degree of collaboration from the reader—what
Coleridge called 'a willing suspension of disbelief'—which
the poet has a right to expect. But the poet must not demand
too much; when poetry, to be poetry, depends upon a certain
way of reading, or upon external music, or upon the imagination of the reader himself, it is really no longer poetry.

Thibaudet, who was sometimes a very penetrating critic
(in his *Histoire de la littérature française de 1789 à nos jours*), has
noted that all these poets end by writing prose, and Paul
Fort is taken as a turning-point. There is much good in
Paul Fort, but is it poetry? Poetry has flooded the novel
and the drama—and perhaps drowned life in all the parts it
has covered. Is Giraudoux drama? Is *Le Grand Meaulnes*
of Alain Fournier a novel? Perhaps both are simply second-
rate poetry.

What can be said of Francis Jammes and of Paul Claudel?
They are the victims of this twilight. Being great Catholics
does not save them—you can be a great Catholic and a minor
poet, just as you can be a staunch rationalist and a bad poet.
And form has much to do with poetry. Both Jammes and
Claudel are really formless, and rely on the originality of their
ideas or impressions to make the reader think they are poets.
But as Lincoln pointed out: 'You cannot fool all the people
all the time.' The people will even rebel against Péguy, and
ask him, for goodness' sake, to shout a little less loud.
'Crier n'est pas chanter,' used to be a precept. Also 'le moi
est haïssable.' All this reasonless and rhymeless poetry
shouts instead of singing, and all these reasonless poets seem
to know too much about themselves that is of little import
to the reader.

So much of French poetry has erred to the right or to the

left. The Madame de Noailles kind of poetry is a useless repetition of old songs that used to be sung better; the Apollinaire kind of poetry is perhaps a formless prelude to future splendours, but that dawn has not broken yet. Not that many lovely lines are not to be found in these vast fields. As in Laforgue and Lautréamont, pleasure will be found fairly often in Moréas, Régnier, and Verhaeren. Some over-rhymed, some not rhymed; those fairly reasonable—none great. Fernand Gregh is a virile counterpart of Madame de Noailles. Perhaps an English-speaking reader should be warned not to take seriously the many one-man schools that appeared in France, and still go on appearing—unanimism with Jules Romains, humanitarianism with Fernand Gregh, even neo-classicism with Moréas. Those are perhaps the best-known cases. Unfortunately, or rather fortunately, they are small traders trying to masquerade as chain-stores—but who wants chain-stores in poetry? Much of Fernand Gregh is good. L'Homme blanc is a great poem. Some Éluard, some Fargue, some Jouve give great pleasure.

> O poet, hold thy peace and be content;

as Wordsworth suggested to their kind long ago.

A NOTE ON PROVENCE

Some readers may be glad of a short mention of Provençal poets. Mistral died in 1914—Mireille had come out in 1859. But Provençal poetry is greater to-day than in Mistral's time, except for the master. It is so different in kind from French poetry that it should be dealt with at length for its own sake. Three poets at least of to-day can be called great: Baroncelli (Blad de Luno, 1910); d'Arbaud (La Bête du Vaccarès, 1926: undoubtedly one of the finest books of this century); and Sully André Peyre, the editor of the periodical Marsyas, which Thibaudet singles out (p. 529) as perhaps the best of the 'petites revues autonomes' (Choix de Poèmes, 1929). The

Provençals have the good habit of printing the French of their own texts on parallel pages. Their noble effort is very pathetic when one considers that at the most they can reach only a few hundred readers in their Provençal. Here is true love of poetry for its own value, regardless of a public. Let us hope at least for the survival of Provençal as a culture language that lives; millions of French people speak dialects akin to the Provençal. A generous educational policy on the part of the French authorities, by making the schools teach Mistralian Provençal as a means of culture, would ensure the life of a noble literature otherwise doomed.

CONCLUSIONS

WHAT ARE THE FRENCH?—LITERATURE AND CHARACTER

WHAT is the place of this period of 1870–1940 in the general history of French literature? How is the period to be judged, compared with previous development? What is there in common between this century and, say, the Romantic period and the Classical period? What are the differences?

Such is the first question that arises from our study: the relationship between the centuries in literature.

If we can define the relationship a second question arises: Can any permanent characteristics of the nation's temperament be deduced from the study of literature? Can it be said, from studying their books, that the French are this or that, at least during a given period—perhaps over the three or four centuries covered adequately by the artistic forms of writing?

General differences emerge fairly clearly from one century to another. It is only after stating what they are that we can look for common ground below the differences.

The greatest French problem is perhaps in the permanent need of the nation to establish some kind of order in the apparently prevalent disorder. French classical literature from Malherbe onwards tries to tidy up and submit to reasonable rules the exuberant growth of the Renaissance. Ronsard, Rabelais, Montaigne are among the giants—but disorderly giants—and from them you cannot learn how to write or how to think. The seventeenth century will bring magnificent order out of magnificent chaos. In the body politic too the era of the absolute king succeeds the tumultuous wars of 1550–90 and the rebellions of the great lords from 1615 to 1640. Richelieu and Mazarin act politically as Malherbe and Descartes act spiritually. This establishment of order is achieved mainly by submitting the individual to the body social. Protestants, great lords, individuals of all kinds must give up their eccentricities, their originalities even, and submit to the common rule. Every one is taught 'le moi est haïssable'; follow the rule; obey the king. The rule is the rule of reason—passion, and especially the passion of love, must yield to the social values. Le Cid has to kill his mistress's father to satisfy the honour of his family. Cinna is forgiven by Augustus for his murderous plans because Rome demands unity, and Cinna becomes a loyal subject. Love goes to merit—is ruled by reason. Polyeucte's wife Pauline, who at first does not love him, soon perceives that he is superior, as a man, to her first lover Sévère, and therefore her deepest affection is gradually transferred to Polyeucte.

At least this should happen—it does happen in Corneille. Racine holds a cheaper estimate of human nature, and shows how frail mankind is, but he acknowledges the rule; and even makes Titus exile Bérénice for reasons of state.

Yet under the prevalent apparent order, disorder is not very far. Racine is Louis XIV's favourite poet; no wonder Racine acknowledges the power of passion. Count Louis XIV's mistresses. There the factors making for disorder are in full sway, and in a field that in literature will be the eternal subject: the field of sexual relationships. Disorder in the sex life is the constant theme from Racine's Phèdre to Proust's Albertine. As a counter-element is the profound power of the family: Louis XIV cannot bear the fact that he has illegitimate children. One of the constant preoccupations of his life is his desire to create a kind of legitimate standing for his bastards: the desire to bring back into an orderly scheme the results of his disorders. The love of women makes for disorder; the love of children makes for order. Even so, in Proust, Swann will marry his *demi-mondaine* mistress whom he has ceased to love, because of the existence of his daughter Gilberte, whom he loves as passionately as Louis XIV loved his bastards.

You might say that after Voltaire and Rousseau—in a battle that is the life of the eighteenth century—disorder won.

The Romantics, from Chateaubriand and Lamartine onwards, are the champions of *le moi*. They rebel against the classical rules, and to them originality, and even eccentricity, is genius. They no longer condemn Phèdre as Racine did; they admire her. *Le moi* is no longer *haïssable*; passion is no longer subject to reason. Passion—love, that is—is now an end in itself, since in passion the self reaches its highest exaltation. Let the social values look after themselves: the Romantic poets count the world well lost if love is won. The sanctity of individual life is a conquest of that Romantic century; life was held in cheap value before the nineteenth century; humanitarianism grows with the rights of the individual and the value of liberty for the private person. Yet the element of order is not very far. All those terribly 'free' and audacious poets really write in exactly the same kind of rhymed couplet as Racine and Boileau, and really they were subjects of Louis Philippe, the king whose motto was as an order given to the nation: 'Enrichissez-vous.' They did. All the great Romantic poets made fortunes, and Hugo managed to run his innumerable love affairs while leading a very successful family life.

Passion rules, aided by imagination. Reason, or at least reasonableness, is not far off.

Then Mallarmé declares that all is changed. Real art, true art, has no connection with reason or with passion. Corneille and Lamartine are equally excommunicated. The values they represent are declared null. Reason? A feeble thing, of no importance; Bergson will put it in its place, and Proust hold celebrations over its grave. Passion? A pure delusion: connected with reason, really. The intellect creates falsehood by its very functioning; the worst falsehood it creates is the delusion that we can love somebody. To begin with, *le moi* does not exist. You look for it in Mallarmé, in Valéry, in Proust, in Gide—it is not there. You may look for it in Zola if you like—you will be wasting your time also; there may be heredity and environment, but the individual *moi* is nothing. Therefore if *le moi* does not exist

how can it love? In the vacuum of human life the master
of illusions, the intellect, and the mistress of delusions, the
imagination, conjure up love out of some abysmal powers
of feeling that somehow (no one knows how) exist in human
beings, and we think, imagine, and feel that we love; but
truly we do not. We merely suffer from delusions.

Yet we write some of the best prose in the whole of
the French tradition and we try to put the whole of life
into fifteen volumes, like Proust, or twenty-seven, like
Jules Romains. Yet Paul Valéry expresses his philosophy of
emptiness and disorder in the most rigorous prosody ever
invented.

A new disorder has been created by Mallarmé and Proust
so that a new order may be constructed out of it. Zola
reveals the atrocities of human nature and the social order
so that they may be corrected.

Throughout the period 1920–40 burns the ardent desire to
see and face and analyse reality at its worst, at its lowest, so
that from this knowledge the power may be won to reach
the highest. A process of denudation of the soul has been
going on since the seventeenth century, but alongside of that
process has lived the desire to find a firm basis on which
to build.

The seventeenth century rejected the exuberance of the
sixteenth, to try and build on reason and law.

The eighteenth century destroyed the old formal religion
on which the seventeenth century had built, to build on
reason and human values.

The nineteenth-century Romantics, going on with the denudation process, threw reason overboard, to reach the layer
of individual rights and imagination, on which they would
build.

The twentieth century overthrows the individual as a basis
on which to build. What is left then?

Why, everything. None of the things that were discarded
has ceased to be. Count them: the *exuberance* of the sixteenth century is still in Céline and in Malraux, and even in

the style and enormous volumes of Proust; the *raison* of the seventeenth century is in Duhamel and Chamson even as in Paul Valéry; the *imagination* of the nineteenth century is in Loti and France and Barrès and Jules Romains. In this period 1920–40 we see the composite picture of the rejection of all previous efforts and simultaneously of the retaining of all previous qualities. A fruition in destruction; really only the old forms are destroyed, the powers are intact, at work creating new forms.

Thus our period appears as, so far, the ultimate phase of the process of denudation in the search for a solid basis on which to build. It cannot be said that the basis has been found; perhaps that search is itself a delusion. But the spiritual powers are certainly being exercised and developed in the double effort of destroying the old and of creating the new—the old is never destroyed, the new never quite achieved. The old disorder is never triumphant, the new order is never attained.

Perhaps the clearest quality, then, of the French is in that passionate love of art that is always evident in a small number of them—a small number, it is true, but revered by the rest. Valéry represents pure art to-day—completely uncommercialized, even as, say, La Fontaine did in the seventeenth century. The one is, as the other was, surrounded by a kind of respect, appreciation, and in many cases, of love, which is truly extraordinary, because their art, in either case, Valéry or La Fontaine, is of an utterly unsentimental kind. But art, in its extremest form, appeals profoundly to the nation. It is certainly connected, in a most ultimate manner, with respect for the artist, which implies, at all times, respect for the liberty of the artist. Louis XIV was most respectful of literature, and took on quite a humble tone—for him—when asking Boileau who was the greatest French poet. When Boileau named Molière, all the absolute monarch could say was: 'Tiens, je ne l'aurais pas cru.' And he held his own very occasional productions in no high esteem.

This desire that art should be free is only an aspect of the larger desire for the freedom of thought: a fundamental characteristic of the French. The extraordinary variety of literary expression, from Mallarmé to Zola, from Proust to Bernanos, from Duhamel to Montherlant, is only possible in a nation where every individual feels fundamentally free to think and to express himself as he likes; and this goes back in time to the Romantic period, to the Voltairean period— when the need and desire for freedom were there in spite of all obstacles—to the Descartes and Pascal period, where greater giants existed, threatened by greater dangers, yet were among the freest spirits of mankind.

Not far from this need of individual liberty is the feeling of the sanctity of the individual, both as a thinking being and as a living being. This is a perhaps more recent acquisition, but Voltaire and Rousseau fought for it, the whole Romantic period was fervent with it, and it has come to stay. *Le Crime gratuit* of Gide is only a wily effort to go against a settled habit of feeling that crime is essentially wrong—as Gide of course proves in his *Voyage au Congo*—a humanitarian plea. Zola rose to heroism in defence of justice and human dignity.

Here perhaps comes in a weakness, and then a counter-weakness of the French: they prefer disorder to injustice— like Goethe, whose great exclamation was ironical since the injustice he preferred to disorder was letting go unhanged a man who did not deserve hanging but whom the mob wanted to hang 'out of justice.' But this preference of the French for disorder lets them down badly, and produces a bad reaction among those that are too sensitive to disorder. Hence the counter-weakness of authoritarianism in France: disorder under Louis XIII, absolutism under Louis XIV; disorder under Danton, execution under Robespierre; disorder under Lamartine; the first Fascism of Napoleon III; and so on. A middle course is difficult to the French. This is well seen in literature, in a period when Céline (disorder made print) is a contemporary of Paul Valéry, a god of order. It is even seen in Valéry alone: a god of order in his lovely form, a god of disorder in his philosophy; or in Gide.

Yet the French know the middle course, too. Molière was of the middle way; Duhamel is of the middle way, and judges his Salavin as Molière judged his Alceste; Montaigne is the middle way.

It must nevertheless be said of the French that perhaps more than their neighbours, they pass too easily from one register to the other, that disorder, order, and the middle way are with them too near each other—in fact, that some section of the nation is always on some track that is divergent from that of some other section. With the French, even the middle way can be a divergent track, as is proved when Molière writes *Tartuffe*, or when Duhamel criticizes America. A difficult people to govern; but let not that be mistaken altogether for a weakness. 'Ordre, contre-ordre, désordre' is a French saying which can be reversed, and become 'désordre, contre-ordre, ordre'—and then many are surprised by what the French can do. Unfortunately, sometimes one is surprised the other way. But in the literature is a symptom of the cause of both strength and weakness; in the evidence that in their love of liberty the French take perhaps too many risks of disorder—and of being exploited by parasites or trapped by enemies.

That is why Anatole France, Barrès, Romains, and many others were so often preoccupied with politics; and their failure to integrate politics in literature is a symptom of the French failure to find stability in the body social. But also it shows deep awareness of the problem—perhaps a condition necessary to some future solution of it. Love of politics is thus a French trait too well marked in the literature.

As for love of woman, it is indeed written large from Mallarmé to Valéry, from Zola to Proust; but in what country and in what literature is it not written large to-day? Let us remember, however, that Fénelon, the good and great archbishop, who was a remarkable literary critic, in his *Lettre à l'Académie* expounds the law that love is not really a fit subject for literature.   What would he say now?   Perhaps we need not insist on a trait in human nature which France's neighbours at some periods have tried to pretend was exclusively a French failing.   The introduction of love of woman into tragedy, which Fénelon objected to even as late as 1700, is paralleled in our time by the introduction of homosexuality, which Proust and Gide have accomplished.   One does not have to be an archbishop to protest—but the thing is done. What will future ages say?   Albertine will live, whatever they say.   The Marquis de Sade is still largely a legend, much spoken of, little read; but Proust and Gide are literary realities. Here again it is of no use to blame the French.   Blame rather the twentieth century.

Which leads to religion, because Fénelon objected really on religious grounds; as do many to-day in the other case.

What of religion in France, as literature tells?

We have had Claudel, Bernanos, Péguy, Mauriac, Maritain. They are not convincing in themselves.   Except perhaps Mauriac—and yet Mauriac also in a reverse way; they protest too much, like the lady in *Hamlet*.   I suspect here, also, the influence of politics.   Bad rhetoric is an effective political weapon; but the romantics also used bad rhetoric, and there is much of the bad romantics in Claudel and Bernanos.   Yet their success is a symptom that many in France have deep religious feelings; here also the nation is divided.   Many more great writers are on the other side: Mallarmé, Zola, are at one here; Anatole France speaks for a vast number of the French, as Voltaire did; Romain Rolland has a middle way (religiosity rather than religion); Malraux and Chamson and Céline and Giono do much more than offset the dubious Montherlant; Barrès is not really a believer; Valéry and Alain are sceptics; Duhamel is at best on the middle way, like Romain Rolland; Bremond is obviously brooding over the past, whatever his own opinions, and despairs of reaching the present—yet he would have found as many mystics as ever in the present.

As in the political field, element and counter-element balance in the religious field; it cannot be said either side dominates; the masses may fluctuate. Yet, in the denudation process we have described, religion fares badly. The eighteenth century has less than the seventeenth, the nineteenth less than the eighteenth, in spite of romantic pretence: Voltaire believed in God more than Lamartine did; Mallarmé believes less than Lamartine; Valéry less than Mallarmé. The run seems to be downhill: Alain believes much less than Montaigne did, sceptic though Montaigne often was. Whatever changes the future may bring—and the symptoms do not really point to an immediate revival, on the whole—the period born under the twin stars Mallarmé-Zola was an irreligious one.

To our first question, then—What is the relationship between our century and the previous ones?—we answer: Fulfilment of desires that were there, destruction of forms and shams, or of old truths become shams.

To our second question—What are the French?—we answer: Lovers of art, lovers of freedom, defenders of the individual, oscillators between order and disorder, as between religion and irreligion; addicts to politics of an erratic kind, ready victims to rhetoric and charlatanism; bold spirits to tackle new questions, especially indecent ones; great lovers of women —of too many women; great lovers of their children—of not enough children. Queerly enough patriotism is not much in evidence in this later literature, and when it appears it produces bad literature.

Many faults—but also many qualities.

But the evidence is somewhat unsatisfactory: literature does not really correspond to life. It is difficult for us to realize this in our own period, but a glance at previous periods will induce caution in us, together with a certain amount of certainty.

The seventeenth-century people were really ultra-romantic. When La Rochefoucauld writes of his mistress, for whose sake he went into rebellion,

> Pour mériter son cœur, pour plaire à ses beaux yeux
> J'ai fait la guerre aux rois, je l'aurais faite aux dieux,

he is most unlike the La Rochefoucauld of *Les Maximes*.   He
is an utter Romantic, ready to attack the gods for the sake of
a woman.   The seventeenth century is, in literature, a time
of law and order; in life, it is the time of d'Artagnan and
the Musketeers.

The fact that Dumas has to go to Louis XIII and Louis XIV
for romance tends to show it was absent in 1830; and it was.
The age of the Romantic poets was the age of *enrichissez-vous*.
Louis Philippe was the most unromantic king of a most unromantic age.   Thus neither the great literature of 1660 nor
the great literature of 1830-40 really reveals what their epochs
were in truth.   Rather the opposite.

Yet look a little more closely.   Seventeenth century—
order?   What of Pascal?   Here we have perhaps the greatest
mind of France.   Where is his order?   He is far above and
beyond order.   Surely God did it on purpose not to let him
put *Les Pensées* in order; because in fact Pascal had a deeply
disorderly mind. He was the profound antithesis to Descartes.

As for 1830–40, what of Balzac?   He is the great anti-
Romantic.   So it is a question of looking in the proper place.
Pascal is a great Romantic, and he, rather than Molière, repre-
sents the true seventeenth century: read Bremond's history
of the mystics.   Balzac is the realist, and he, rather than
Lamartine, represents the 1830s.

What will history say of the 1930s?   We cannot tell yet.
But, judging by the history of the past, we can see two elements of unprecedented good: intellectual courage and love of
the truth.   Make for the truth, however bitter; and publish
what you find.   Gide.   Proust.   Zola.   Face up to the worst.
Lamartine never did.   Bossuet never did.   However hypocritical we may still be, no age has been less hypocritical than
ours.   No age has loved the truth more.   In no age has a
man like Zola—rather a mediocre man otherwise, mark that
—written a document like *J'accuse* for love of justice and
truth.   In no age has a man like Proust so fearlessly explored
the self and faced its complete annihilation.   The courage of
Proust in his sphere is comparable to the courage of Zola.

And the Zola of *J'accuse* is only the Zola of *L'Assommoir*: the truth about the drunkard workman is hard to tell for a man of the Left like Zola. But Zola tells the truth, as he sees it; even as Gide does; or, higher still, even as Valéry does when he says: 'Nous autres civilisations, nous savons maintenant que nous sommes mortelles.'

Therefore the literature from 1870 to 1940 is probably a better mirror of life as it was during the period than literature in 1830 or in 1660. So we can have some confidence in a diagnosis derived from literature. Another fact: the number of great names, the number of great books. Perhaps no single giant towers over the period. Proust is at best but a very sickly kind of giant, and Valéry is more a spirit, perhaps a ghost, than a giant; and Duhamel is rather a man than anything else. But the number of names: Mallarmé, Zola, Loti, Barrès, France, Jules Romains, Duhamel, Bernanos, Mauriac, Rostand, Rolland, Gide, Proust, Valéry, Supervielle, Alain, Céline, not to mention even a dozen others, nor the relatively young who are yet mostly in the future; in 1830, in 1660, you could not mention so many. Perhaps we are over-impressed by our contemporaries? But round about 1700 there was 'la querelle des anciens et des modernes,' and the then *modernes* could not mention as many names as that. And Voltaire has put a list of good writers at the end of *Le Siècle de Louis XIV*, and except for the very greatest names we can produce a better list, a longer list, of good books. Some of Voltaire's chosen men had a name merely for one poem, and not such a good one either.

So even allowing for our lack of perspective, we can hold that we have lived in a very rich period in French literature; and as varied as it is rich. The nation, therefore, is very far from being tired or in any way near exhaustion. So rich a field in the present is bound to have great reserves underground, and this simple remark allows us to cherish the highest hopes yet of the future.

The turbulence is that of youth; there are no signs of old age.

BIBLIOGRAPHICAL INDEX

Page references in the text are given at the end of each entry

This is not meant as a complete bibliography, but merely as a list of books to read first.

GENERAL BIBLIOGRAPHY

ALBERT THIBAUDET. *Histoire de la littérature française de 1789 à nos jours.* The most complete book on the subject; goes roughly as far as 1936. Both systematic in its classifications and (often) erratic in judgment.

LANSON AND TUFFREAU. *Histoire de la littérature française.* Deals with Proust, Gide, and Valéry. Academic in the best sense: well balanced in judgment and as objective as possible. Has an excellent list of authors and books from 1880 to 1930.

R. LALOU. *Histoire de la littérature française contemporaine.* Stops at 1920.

A. BILLY. *Histoire de la littérature française contemporaine.* Stops at 1927. Both this and the previous book reflect rather antiquated points of view, and many of the authors they mention have really ceased to be widely known.

MARCEL BRAUNSCHVIG. *La Littérature française contemporaine.* Is presented as a school book, with many texts. It is an invaluable book, full of historical information not to be found elsewhere. It goes down to 1931, but will certainly be brought up to date as soon as possible.

DENIS SAURAT. *Tendances* (Le Monde moderne, Paris), 1928.
Modernes (Denoël et Steele, Paris), 1935.
Perspectives (Stock, Paris), 1938.